Family Tales

Rewriting the Stories
That Made You Who You Are

Rewriting the Stories
That Made You Who You Are

James Osterhaus

InterVarsity Press
Downers Grove, Illinois

InterVarsity Press® is the book-publishing division of InterVarsity Christian Fellowship®, a student movement active on campus at hundreds of universities, colleges and schools of nursing in the United States of America, and a member movement of the International Fellowship of Evangelical Students. For information about local and regional activities, write Public Relations Dept., InterVarsity Christian Fellowship, 6400 Schroeder Rd., P.O. Box 7895, Madison, WI 53707-7895.

Library of Congress Cataloging-in-Publication Data

Osterhaus, James P.
   Family tales: rewriting the stories that made you who you are /
James Osterhaus.
        p.   cm.
   Includes bibliographical references.
   ISBN 0-8308-1996-7 (alk. paper)
   1. Family—Religious aspects—Christianity.   2. Family—Religious
life.   3. Family psychotherapy.   I. Title.
   BV4526.2.O87   1997
   248.4—dc21   96-36846
                                                                              CIP

20   19   18   17   16   15   14   13   12   11   10   9   8   7   6   5   4   3   2   1

13   12   11   10   09   08   07   06   05   04   03   02   01   00   99   98   97

Introduction

The Story You've Known

It was the phone call that all parents dread.

"Reverend Simmons, this is the police."

Bill Simmons gripped the receiver, his hand beginning to shake.

"We didn't have to call you. Your son Billy is over eighteen and considered an adult. But we wanted you to know that he has been arrested and charged with breaking and entering and possession of a firearm."

"Yes, officer. Ah—thank you, officer. I'll be right there." Bill Simmons hung up the phone and slumped down in a nearby kitchen chair, his thoughts racing, his heart beginning to beat fast. The family drama was climaxing, but this scene had been building for many years.

"Bill, what's the matter? Who was that?" Bill's wife Mary asked.

"The police. They have Billy. He's been arrested for breaking and entering." Bill decided he would not mention the part about possession until later.

Mary slumped in a chair, face in her hands, and sobbed.

The Simmons family was seen as a pillar of the small Shenandoah Valley community where they resided. Bill had run a successful concrete business and had been active in service clubs and coaching.

Mary had been a regular volunteer at their church. When Bill finally sold his business and went to seminary, everyone agreed that he would make an excellent minister—compassionate, clear-thinking, honest. He and Mary now put in long hours not only at the church but also in ministries to the down and out, organizing a local tutoring program and also a crisis pregnancy center in a nearby city. Their oldest daughter Julie had been at the center of school life since she had begun school and had climaxed her career there as head cheerleader and homecoming queen. Marie, the next daughter, had had some difficulties, but people assumed she lived in the long shadow of her sister.

But Billy was a different matter. He'd found ways to stir up trouble since he was a youngster—smashing pumpkins at Halloween, throwing rocks at passing cars, torturing a neighbor's pet. Bill and Mary had tried all they knew to get this wayward boy under control. They'd been in counseling on a number of occasions. They had gotten the youth director at the church to pay special attention to Billy. They'd sent him to camps, had him tutored. Bill had been Billy's coach in any sport he chose.

What really hurt for Bill was that when he decided to go into the ministry, Billy was at the ceremony with beer on his breath, acting obnoxious to everyone around. "I guess he's the cross I must bear," Bill would say, disguising the pain from everyone.

Billy had gone on to college but had done virtually nothing during his three semesters there. Older sister Marie, who was at the same school, sent back reports that Billy was in the wrong crowd and might have drifted into drugs. After school, he had come back to the valley, attempted a number of low-paying jobs and continued to hang out with the wrong crowd. Now had come the phone call from the police.

This family's story continues to unfold, even as the family weathers this storm and the children grow and leave home. I came to play a small part in this family story of Bill and Mary, a story that will unfold throughout the pages of this book.

Why a Story?

I've taken some time over the last year to learn how to understand and write stories. I've looked at how a story is fashioned, how plot is developed, how characters are introduced and cultivated, the way dialogue unfolds. I've become fascinated with stories as they've existed down through the centuries. And as I studied stories, I began to see how our lives are really the unfolding of a unique story.

I began to think of my own family story. I was raised in a very middle-class family in a suburb of Washington, D.C. My parents were stable and trustworthy. I have an older sister and brother. I thought, as I tracked through school, that I'd end up a minister. But during college I became intrigued by psychology, and I ended up a counselor. Not much there in that story, I thought.

But wait, there's so much more to this story. My father had married late (at age thirty) because of financial uncertainty brought on by the Depression (he'd turned twenty-one only months before the stock-market crash in 1929).

Born in Germany, he had immigrated to the United States before World War I with his family, settling in New York. He then followed his older siblings to Washington, D.C., in search of work when he reached adulthood.

Mom had been raised in northern Virginia. Her family stretched back generations in the area, all the way to the late 1600s. Her grandfather had ridden cavalry in the Civil War, then come home, resumed his career as a carpenter, built a small Baptist church and later pastored it for a short time.

Mom and Dad came together in marriage just before the outbreak of World War II. Theirs was an uncertain, dangerous world. My sister and brother were both born during the war—my sister well before the Allies gained the upper hand. I was born shortly after the war, at the beginning of the baby boom generation.

But the story is so much deeper and richer than even this. My parents beheld each of us children through different lenses, different hopes and expectations. My sister, the creative musician, was pushed into piano, clarinet and later organ. She majored in music and now is assistant music director in a church. My brother was seen through the lens of competition; he was the athlete. He's now a minister. I was seen more for my brains, I think. I have the Ph.D. and write books.

And the story can be told in other ways. There were emotional tones and issues that periodically cycled through the family. As we developed our personal stories, the family story has been altered, and society's story continues to ebb and flow around us. But that initial family story still exerts a powerful influence on who I am and what I have come to be.

Everyone grows up within a unique family story. Like me, you may be a part of a number of intersecting families, each with its own unique story.

There's the family story I originally experienced, the one I described above, of my mother and father who gave birth to me and raised me. (You, on the other hand, may have been raised by parents different from those who brought you into the world.)

My present nuclear family, made up of my wife Marcy and my children Mandy, Peter and Ben, presents another story. There's also my wife's family of origin with its unique story—my mother and father-in-law and the story they continue to write after nearly fifty years. My brother and sister and their family stories. My sister-in-law and her family story. Aunts, uncles, cousins and their family stories. My nephew got married a few years ago and now has a baby, so his is another story in the constellation of family stories.

Families have been looked at, studied, dissected and worried over since the dawn of time. We do this because we innately know how important the family is to us.

But why consider families through the lens of story? Actually, people are natural storytellers. One theorist, R. C. Schank, states that all human memory is story-based. Our minds aren't set up to understand raw logic. Furthermore, he states, not every experience makes a good story. But if it does, the experience will be easier to remember.[1] Stories give us the critical links we need to understand events in terms of what we already know.

We live according to stories, we think according to stories, we make decisions according to stories. With stories we organize our experiences, making sense of the endless stream of sensory data that constantly assaults us. Our communication is limited to the number of stories we know to tell. Conversation is reminding each other of stories. The world can be seen as a set of stories we use to shape our view of ourselves and our reality.[2] Stories give meaning to the past, organize our present, and focus our future.

The initial story that shaped us was the family story that unfolded in our living rooms, kitchens and bedrooms. The plot thickened around holidays and vacations. Characters were introduced and developed as children were born, in-laws came to visit, grandparents moved in to live and die. The power of our family stories continues to pervade our lives.

Why This Book?

This book has been designed to help you get a better understanding of the particular family stories in which you have lived.

We'll look backward to see and understand the family stories that surrounded and involved you, gave you definition and sustained you. I'll give you some tools to help you search out the story patterns that were operating as your story was written.

We'll also note the unique dimensions of your family story. You will begin to see the themes that were present, the dialogue that was used, the way each family character was introduced and shaped to fit into the family plot as it unfolded.

Why do this? you may be asking yourself. *The story happened— what's the purpose of digging it up now? Do you think I need to blame someone for things that happened to me?*

First, let me say that blaming parents or others for your present difficulties is not only not helpful in your present and future development but even harmful. I assume that your parents, no matter how badly they managed things when you were young, were doing the best job they knew how to do in the circumstances in which they found themselves as they wrote the family story (though instances of severe abuse and neglect will require careful consideration and forgiveness). The impact on you may have been very negative and destructive. And rewriting that story will be imperative. But blaming parents is not the goal—quite the contrary. God uses all the mistakes, abuses and poor judgments that befell us in our family stories to shape us into the characters he wants us to be. And knowing the story he wants to write on our lives is critical.

Second, I want to give you a sense of why you are the person you are today (the character you exhibit in the stories you inhabit), why you respond as you do in certain situations, why you act, think and feel the way you do.

Third, I want to help you discern places in the story that need rewriting. That's right: the story can be edited, revised, rewritten. You don't have to just live out the story that was first handed to you. God would have us conform our stories to the unique story he is writing for each of us. In conforming our stories to his story for us, we enter into a partnership with him—a partnership in editing our story.

When you are finished with this book, you should be able to understand how your stories have been written—your personal story, the family story from which you came and the family story you are currently writing. You should also be a more astute and discerning writer as with God's constant assistance, you go about fashioning the stories you are currently creating in your marriage, your family, your work associations and your walk with the Lord.

Your Unique Family Story
Have you ever wondered:
☐ How come I can't seem to stay in a relationship with someone for more then a few months?
☐ Why am I so optimistic, even when things go wrong?
☐ Why do I always seem to become fearful when authority figures are around?
☐ Why do I always feel I have to please everyone?

☐ How come I can never seem to complete anything I begin?

☐ Why do I always seem to let others walk all over me?

You've probably asked these or other similar questions as you've looked at your life story. As you continue to look into your family story, I think you'll find that your responses to life, your way of conducting yourself, your whole lifestyle and outlook are there because of the way your particular family story developed.

As we have already said, each of us comes *from* a unique family story and is currently *in* unique family stories. Within those family stories, each of us played a particular part (or parts) that furthered the plot of each of those stories. Not only do we play roles in these stories, but in many ways we are also writers, or at least cowriters, of the stories that we help act out.

No one else in your family story tells the story exactly the same way you do. In storywriting this is called "point of view." Everyone lives out the story from his unique point of view (perspective). All the versions of the family story stem from attempts by the various family characters to adapt to the unique plot line as it unfolds in the family. Members play different roles, elicit different responses from other members and therefore interpret situations differently.

Each individual version of the family story is told with the teller as the protagonist (hero). In your version all other family characters are subordinated to your acting and reacting, mere role players in your personal unfolding story. Each individual cast member (parents, siblings) also has his or her own individual story which is interwoven into the family story.

If you think about it, you may find yourself confused as to how much of your story was "true" and how much was false. *Did this really happen in the way I perceived it?* People come to me with many pages of their story missing. They can't seem to remember what happened, but they fear that something went terribly wrong when they were young. Within those missing pages of the story are secrets to present distresses, poor relationships and bad decisions.

The story of your family, and those who created it, helped mold you into who you are today. Just as an author of a novel molds his characters, shaping them (and, curiously, they in turn begin to influence the author as he writes), so the authors of our stories shaped and were shaped by us. We'll discuss this more later.

Knowing your own particular family story, how it came to be and how the characters acted goes far in helping you change many of the scripts you've come to live by. Family stories are rarely open for inspection and rewriting, unless people work to become aware of the unfolding story. We're part of those stories, going about playing our roles, unaware of the process.

As I talk about the family story, I realize that there are actually several interlocking stories that are unfolding simultaneously. There's my own personal story, which is written in the context of the family story. The family story is being written in the context of our culture's story, and that story is written in the context of God's Story. Each story can be seen as its own entity, yet each story also draws from the surrounding story. We could diagram it like figure 1.

This book will focus on the family story. However, we will also touch on the other stories as they have impact on the family story at any given point.

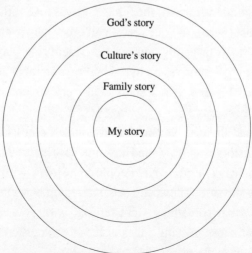

Figure 1. Interlocking stories

Your Family Story and God's Story

The Bible is filled with family stories. In fact, much of God's Word comes to us in the form of story. It's no accident that the Bible picks up the family image as it unfolds the ultimate Story of God's grace. He is the Father who loves us. As we receive the salvation he offers, we are adopted into his family. In another family metaphor, we as the church become the bride of Christ.

To explain his story to us, Jesus told of a man who has two sons. One son asks for and receives his share of the inheritance, which he promptly squanders on loose living. He ends up in a muddy pen competing with pigs for his meals. Then he decides to return to his father to throw himself on his mercy and become his servant. Father sees the boy coming, runs to him, restores his place in the family and starts a celebration. This wayward younger son stands aghast, uncomprehending of his father's love *(I thought I'd missed out because I was so bad)*.

Meanwhile his older brother slaves in the fields, hoping to earn his father's love. When he hears of the party thrown in behalf of his prodigal brother, he's livid: "How could you, Father? I'm the one who slaves to please you!"

"But son," the father interrupts, "certainly you don't slave in the fields to earn my love. All that I have is yours."

Now it's the older brother's turn to stand aghast. He too has misunderstood the love of the father *(I thought I had to earn it)*.

Through the ages, people have been readily able to see and understand stories and images like this one. God seems somehow remote and unknowable until he's seen in terms of the unfolding family story. Then all at once my eyes open, and I can understand him much better.

But it's also important to understand that we are not just dealing in metaphor here. God intends to rewrite the story of our lives, to restructure that story so that it is more in keeping with the way he originally intended our life story to be.

The Exercises

I've interspersed exercises throughout this book to assist you as you journey through your family's story. I know that will make the book take longer to get through, but I think you'll get more out of your reading if you set the book down and do the exercises. I'll also tell you how you can involve other people at various times when this would be helpful. After completing the exercises, you should have a fairly complete story of your family. You should also be able see those areas of your story that will need rewriting.

There are several ways you can do the exercises. I think it would be most helpful if you got a spiral notebook in which you can make entries as you write your family story. As part of this emerging story you may wish to include family photos, letters or other mementos. I love to write, so that's what I would do. But you may not be comfortable writing, and you may not want to use writing as your method of doing the exercises. If that is the case, don't worry.

If you're more a hands-on learner, there will be things to manipulate and draw. And if you are more orally inclined, I have given alternatives for talking through the exercises. (You'll get just as much out of it if you explain specific chapters of your family story to someone, or recite to yourself what has happened to you.) If you happen to be more visually oriented, you could get doll figures that represent your family and act out the exercises.

You may choose to go through this book by yourself, and that's fine. It would also be helpful to sit down with your entire family, or parts of your family that can be assembled, and approach the book as a group. Or you may be able to find several friends, singles or couples, with whom you can discuss the questions and results of the exercises.

I hope this book will be redemptive for you, that in seeing the story of your family and your life as it was written, you will be able to make significant changes that will draw you closer to the story God would have you live out to his glory.

1

A
Well-Written
Story

B *ill and Mary Simmons* sat in the police station, waiting for word of their son's fate. Both hoped and prayed they would not be recognized. Their minds drifted to when they had first come together as man and wife, and when their two daughters Julie and Marie were born. Then their joy when Billy was born. He seemed to complete the family perfectly.

Bill and Mary had both striven to be perfect parents. Devotions every evening after dinner. Church on Sunday, sometimes during midweek. They had read every Christian book they could find on being good parents and had made conscious efforts to emulate what was written. They had also been to Marriage Encounter and other church-sponsored retreats and conferences in an attempt to keep their marriage healthy.

Bill had made a concerted effort to be with his family. Yes, he had become heavily involved with his company, especially during those early years when it was so important for him to make a good showing. But no one would accuse him of being a bad father, or Mary of being an unfit mother. Their family always looked so healthy, so normal, so ideal.

The Simmons family is a family that is clearly in trouble. Thankfully, most of you who are reading this book have less dramatic family stories than the unfortunate Simmons clan. But every family story has healthy plot lines and unhealthy plot lines. We all came from family stories that succeeded in certain ways and failed miserably in others. Before we continue with the story of Bill and Mary Simmons, let's clarify what exactly is involved in a successful family story.

Characters in the Healthy Family
Successful family stories that I have seen begin with the characters that inhabit those stories. These individuals display certain traits that contribute to the unfolding story in such a way that all parts of that story fit together more perfectly. The traits for fathers and mothers are not necessarily completely different or mutually exclusive.

Fathers. I have just returned from a Promise Keepers weekend held in a stadium in Washington, D.C. There I joined with over fifty thousand other men to sing, pray and hear what God is saying to Christian men around the country. It seems that a major shift is taking place in our culture, in both secular and religious circles. Men are stepping out of the shadows and back onto center stage in all the important relationships outside the workplace.

Actually men stepped *into* the shadows at home when they went off to work in the Industrial Revolution. No longer was their primary work site at home. They worked long hours at another location, and when they returned home their energies were largely spent. Now we quite possibly could be seeing men stepping back out of the shadows and taking their role in the family seriously.

What are fathers for, anyway? What did God have in mind when he fashioned these particular creatures? Debates rage as to what are the unique features of a man and a father as opposed to a woman and a mother. Men and women, though equal before God, express their humanity differently. This difference is obviously physical but also has intellectual and psychological ramifications.[1] These differences are expressed as the man becomes father and the woman becomes mother. Many of the traits I list for fathers or mothers are easily translated to the other parent as well, yet each parent fashions his or her own particular role uniquely according to his or her own way of seeing the world.

1. My father names me. Much of who I am, and the way that I experience myself, comes from my father's input. Naming, in our culture, involves passing on a surname. But it also involves a deeper "naming" as the father defines the essence of what he sees in his child. ("She's so gregarious." "He'll be a real thinker, that son of mine.")

2. My father accepts me. Shaquille O'Neal, the then twenty-year-old center, was playing through his stellar rookie year in the NBA with a seven-year, forty-million-dollar contract. Joe Gargiolla, the sports commentator, asked him, "What really gets you excited?"

The young Orlando Magic center answered, "When my father calls me and tells me he loves me."

My father listens to me. Acceptance begins with the listening ear. Fathers who write healthy family stories are fathers who take time and listen to their children, beginning in infancy. What their children have to say—even small children—is important to them.

My father also points out those areas in my life that are adequate, acceptable and pleasing. He realizes that it is ultimately God who is writing his children's stories, not him.

3. My father guides me and corrects me. By his example and by his direct interventions, a father helps write his children's stories. He corrects sternly but lovingly, but he also instructs and leads me down paths that are ultimately productive to his children.

4. My father provides for me. Unfortunately, during the last century, fathers' role became depersonalized and redefined as a provider—that man who goes off in the morning and returns in the evening with a paycheck. But the father has a critical role to provide for his family materially (he makes money to live on), socially (he initiates and/or participates as the family interacts with the surrounding community), mentally (he stimulates family members to think new thoughts and consider alternative options), and spiritually (he is a priest to his wife and family, guiding them to focus on the Lord Jesus).

5. My father protects me. This is not just physical protection, although that is periodically needed. In a broader sense, fathers writing healthy family stories protect their wives' and children's dignity and honor.

6. My father gives me freedom. Without a father on the scene, a mother can become too close to her children, especially her daughters. Fathers are crucial to helping children separate from the family and gain their own personhood. A large percentage of children get their first jobs as a direct result of their father's influence (that is, the father can be a *sponsor*).[2]

7. My father pushes me forward. Researchers have found that fathers more than mothers are the ones who encourage their children to take risks and reach for achievement.

In healthy families, fathers are prominent. They've stepped out of the shadows of the home and made their families a priority. As leaders, fathers see themselves as sources of character development for their children: *I must create an atmosphere where everyone can grow to their full potential in Christ.*

So how can fathers do all of the things they are supposed to do? By being men of character, men who through action and decision have developed moral and spiritual rectitude. Stephen Covey states that we need men of character and integrity, not men obsessed with image and technique. The father of character is solid at the foundation. A foundation of integrity involves maturity or completeness (the mature individual has reached the goal of the process of personal growth), wholeness, honesty and sincerity.

In the movie *A Man for All Seasons* Thomas More has taken a stand on his spiritual principles and finds himself in conflict with the king. His daughter Meg tries to get him to swear a false oath to King Henry, but More rebukes her gently: "When a man takes an oath, Meg, he's holding his own self in his hands. Like water. And if he opens his fingers then, he needn't hope to find himself again."

Mothers. A passage in an old play (author and title unknown) said it this way: "The mother in her office holds the key of the soul; and she it is who stamps the coin of character and makes the being who would be a savage, but for her gentle cares, a Christian man! Then crown her the queen of the world."

Somehow, all of us know that mothers are a critical glue that holds everything together in society. That may be too strong a statement, for certainly we are aware of the critical contributions of fathers to the developing child. But mothers have a special role because they first carry us within their body, then deliver us to the world and become our primary nurturers and teachers.

Still, it is important to note that the first three chapters of Genesis do not teach that motherhood is the primary responsibility of the woman; her first responsibility is partnering with the man.[3] Successful mothers and fathers are people who have learned how to be partners together, people who have learned how to make that partnership a priority in their unfolding family stories.

What are mothers for? This too is a controversial question today. Is her primary role to be guardian of the home sphere? Is she equal in every way to her husband in wage earning? Certainly several important characteristics can be enumerated.

1. My mother brings me into the world and points me toward maturity. She is a constant in my life, one on whom I can depend. Through her I learn that the world is safe and that I can trust both my own instincts and the actions of other trustworthy people.

2. My mother deliberately creates conditions in the home that stimulate me to grow to my full potential as a responsible person. Mothers in well-written family stories don't do everything for everyone. They know that their job is to work themselves out of a job. As a result, they don't remove all the obstacles. They realize that trying, failing, suffering pain and learning how to pick ourselves up and start over until we accomplish things on our own is critical to the growth of self-esteem. Therefore they turn responsibilities over to each child as he or she demonstrates capability.

3. My mother nurtures me and gives me a feeling of belonging and being loved. She realizes that the formula for self-esteem is not just

challenge and accomplishment but also the presence of nurture. She knows how to balance the two also—to make demands of her children, to let them suffer pain, but then to give tender care when this is called for. One family theorist has made the interesting observation that as adults we care for ourselves in the very same manner in which our mothers cared for us when we were infants.[4] The implications of this are profound: we treat ourselves sadistically or lovingly, coldly or tenderly, critically or sympathetically based on our mother's handling of us.

Researcher Daniel Stern notes a process he calls "attunement" whereby the mother meets the infant's displays of various emotions with empathy and acceptance. This gives the infant the feeling of being emotionally connected and understood, in addition to knowing that he is allowed to express a full range of emotion.[5]

4. My mother teaches me the truth and points me in the right paths. Mothers point us toward what is good and true and right. They do not hesitate to take a stand for what they believe to be right.

5. My mother allows me to develop the unique traits and personality that God has given me. She is able, from my birth, to note my unique characteristics and to help me develop my potentials to their fullest.

Successful mothers are also women of character. The writer of the Proverbs has written a poem of amazing beauty to describe the woman of "noble character" (Prov 31:10-31). Though this poem can be misused to saddle women with an unbearable load of expectations, it is instructive that the value of the woman described springs from her character of godly wisdom that is beneficial both to her family and to the larger community. (Many scholars feel that this poem in fact captures the ideals of wisdom that are enumerated throughout the Proverbs and are not to be taken as normative for women alone.)

Because the healthy mother is a woman of character, who she is as a person far overshadows how much she knows about mothering. As a pastime I enjoy reading biographies. I guess I've read hundreds by now. At the foundation of the vast majority of people who have risen to prominence is a woman of virtue, often a woman of amazing spiritual strength, who undergirds her family with her godly character.

Children. In well-written family stories, children display health on mental, physical, emotional and spiritual levels.[6]

1. Healthy children believe in themselves. This requires confidence, decisiveness, firmness and vigor (as opposed to emotionality, sensitivity, frailty and submissiveness).

2. Healthy children are emotionally intelligent, restraining emotional excesses without dampening emotional expression. This is what the Scriptures seem to mean with references to being "temperate" or "self-controlled." The temperate person is able to

☐ know her own emotions

☐ manage her emotions

☐ motivate herself, marshaling emotions to achieve a goal

☐ recognize emotions in others

☐ handle relationships[7]

3. Healthy children are willing to take risks. This requires daring, courage, adventurousness, robustness, decisiveness and confidence (as opposed to passivity, helplessness, vacillation and excessive refinement).

4. Healthy children display autonomy. This requires assertiveness, courage and power (as opposed to impotence, childlikeness, excessive connectedness to others and a need to be protected).

5. Healthy children are interdependent. This requires trust (as opposed to fearfulness). Interdependent children know and appreciate their primary dependence on God. Then they are able to form lasting relationships of mutual trust with other people.

Those who develop the most interpersonal polish exhibit skills at

☐ organizing groups (essential skill of a leader): initiating and coordinating the work of a group of people

☐ negotiating solutions (essential skill of a mediator): mediating conflict as it flares up

☐ personal connection: recognizing and responding to the feelings of others in an appropriate manner

☐ social analysis: noticing and understanding the feelings, motives and concerns of other people[8]

Relationships in the Well-Written Family Story

Family stories are populated by individuals who relate to one another. These relationships form the context in which individual characters can grow and develop within the family.

Marriage. Someone once said, "When all else is destroyed, what will remain is God's Word and relationships." At the base of all earthly relationships is the family. And at the base of family relationships is a marriage.

This is not to say that everyone must be married. Some families may be broken by divorce or death, but remain families nonetheless. Yet marriage is a foundational relationship. So what constitutes a healthy, well-written marital story?

1. Healthy couples are composed of two people who make and keep promises. God makes and keeps his promises. God made us and put us in relationship with himself and each other. All of these relationships are interrelated. Our relationships with each other are modeled on God's relationship with us.

☐ Marriage is foundational to family, which is foundational to community, nation and society.

☐ Promise is foundational to marriage. Marriage, family and society form an upside-down pyramid whose base must be held in place by promise. Professor Lewis Smedes from Fuller Seminary has described promises well: promises reach into the future and create safe places. When I make a promise, I form a bond, tying myself to others and making us secure. The promises we make to each other give birth to the trust we have in each other.[9] When we marry, we promise "to have and to hold, from this day forward, till death us do part." Healthy couples keep those promises.

2. Healthy couples are composed of people who have left their families of origin. We've all heard the verse in Genesis 3 about leaving parents and cleaving to one's spouse. Jesus reiterated this point. Why is this important? "Leaving" is an emotional separation, not so much a physical one. When I'm too close to something or someone I can't maintain my perspective or see from different angles. I will tend to

center on particular flaws or assets without seeing the whole picture. As I get distance, my perspective changes. I learn to see my parents for the good and bad they did in my life.

My separateness allows me then to enter into a close bond with another. The paradox of healthy marriage is that two separate, well-defined individuals can enter into a bond much more closely and fully, while still maintaining their individuality.

3. Healthy couples know how to serve one another and share power with each other. Each partner in a healthy couple knows the importance of serving the other. In fact, partnership is what characterizes the healthy couple as they approach life. Once this orientation has been firmly established in the minds of the husband and wife, issues of power seem never to arise, or when they do, these are easily defused. I believe that when the smoke finally clears in debates over the role of power, authority and headship in marriage, the concept of spouses' being partners together will be the most important element left.

4. Healthy couples keep clear boundaries between themselves and others. A boundary is anything that marks a limit or border. It implies a restriction. Boundaries *define* in the sense that a boundary shows who is and who isn't in an organization (such as a family or a club) and also shows what makes a person distinctive from others (my ideas, my feelings, my dreams) and how that person should act. *This is who I am apart from who you are. And this is how I should act.* Boundaries also *protect* priorities.

Boundaries are critical to forming and maintaining a marriage. Each partner must have a boundary around the self *(this is who I am as opposed to you; these are my thoughts, my feelings, my desires).* Sounds simple, but many people have not developed a good sense of self and have trouble maintaining their own ideas, feelings and judgments.

When two people join in marriage, they also need a boundary around their relationship that restricts others from gaining access in important ways. Certain physical, emotional and intellectual activities are off limits to outsiders—even to their parents and their children.

5. Healthy couples know what love is all about. The ancients had

several words for love, which make sense, for love presents many faces. The Hebrews used the word *hesed* to express covenant love, a loyalty to promises made. This word roughly parallels the New Testament idea of *grace,* a love that goes beyond the lovability of the person and loves because of prior promises. If promises are the glue that holds relationships together, then love is that special ingredient in the glue that makes things stick tight.

Love that binds a healthy couple together finds its basis in promise, not in feelings for the person loved. Though I lose my feelings for the person, I can go on loving, precisely because I made promises long ago to do just that.

6. Healthy couples are composed of two people who know how to be intimate. There are several critical aspects of intimacy:

☐ I must be sure of who I am—emotionally, intellectually, spiritually, physically (separated and bounded).

☐ I must know I'm safe before I can draw close. It is important to learn to distinguish between real danger and the reflexive fears that develop in untrusting people. Untrusting people tend to overmonitor and to mobilize themselves immediately in the face of perceived threat (much of which is no threat at all). They are like a smoke detector that's always stuck in the alarm mode, even when there is no smoke.

☐ Then I must know how to draw close. Many do not know how to discuss their feelings, their deepest longings and dreams. Or if they know how to share in this area, they don't know how to be intimate intellectually or creatively. Researchers find that men and women have different conversation styles. Intimate couples learn to understand each other's "language" and communicate across barriers.

☐ Intimacy has many facets (sexual, emotional, intellectual, aesthetic, recreational). All couples find that they are adept at certain types of intimacy and not so adept at others.

7. Healthy couples are composed of two people who know the place of passion. The physical component of the relationship is the most exciting dimension, and the most dangerous. Passion is highly possessive. It is the longing and craving between a man and a woman.

Passion leads to physiological arousal, creating an intense desire to unite with the loved one and finally to a desire to penetrate and be penetrated. Unlike intimacy, it develops quickly.

So why is there passion, and the sex drive that goes hand in hand with it? At times it can be so pleasurable, at other times so annoying or even dangerous. Passion drives us out of isolation toward each other. In this way it helps us form lasting, permanent, committed relationships, for we realize that we live dependent on each other and desperately need each other. The male and female know themselves only in relation to each other, because they are made for each other. They experience a deep desire to come together.

In the act of sex we symbolically uncover our inner selves, our deepest fears and yearnings.[10] Obviously such mutual disclosure and acceptance are not for a moment's delight, but for a lifetime of committed relationship.

8. Healthy couples know how to disagree without being disagreeable. Relationship involves conflict. Absence of conflict does not represent health; a couple who proudly announce, "We haven't had a fight in thirty years!" are not a healthy couple. The goal is not absence of conflict but proper management of conflict. Conflict leads to resolution. When there is an absence of conflict, there invariably are issues lying under the surface that have not been resolved.

9. Healthy couples constantly monitor and recalibrate the expectations that each has of the other. Unconscious, uncommunicated, unrealistic, unreasonable expectations are dangerous. They lurk just under the surface, weaving agendas for the spouse. Other expectations are conscious but are not articulated.

Marriage is fraught with the most powerful expectations—and the most hidden ones—of any relationship. Our most powerful expectations come from our sense of woundedness. For I expect to gain from my partner the healing that I have thus far been unable to obtain.

The healthy couple sets aside time periodically to take inventory of expectations. Expectations that are no longer necessary, valid or useful are discarded. Clifford Sager, a marriage theorist, says this process is much like a contract negotiation,[11] where two parties (husband and wife) spread out their expectations before each other and dicker over what the nature and direction of the marriage will be. "I want us to be closer emotionally," the wife offers. "Okay," the husband counters, "but I want more time to pursue a hobby by myself."

Parenting. In well-written family stories, parenting is a shared task. Moms and dads both participate in bringing children to maturity. Though they don't always agree on every point, parents find ways to agree on the major issues and learn how to disagree agreeably.

There are two indispensable ingredients to raising children who are mature and successful: *support* and *challenge*. Support means that first the parents are present and involved in the lives of their children. These parents then respect their children and pay attention to their physical, emotional, mental and spiritual needs. Challenge means that parents push their children to the edge of their capabilities.[12]

Taking support and challenge together, we arrive at a chart which shows positive and negative factors in parenting that lead to well-written or not so well-written family stories.

Positive Factor	Negative Factor
Acceptance and warmth toward the child (support)	Rejection of the child: "You are not OK as a person"
Firmness in setting limits and discipline	Leniency in setting limits
Respect for the child's autonomy: the parent turns responsibilities over to the child as he is able to perform them (challenge)	Control: the parent needs to direct all the child's activities no matter how competent the child has become

Single parenting. Often single parents get lost in the shuffle, so let's make several points about single parenting that are crucial to keep in mind. Single parents who are writing good family stories develop several particular skills.

1. They constantly monitor expectations. They realize that single parenting is extremely difficult, and they tend to expect craziness at times.

2. They are able to grieve the loss of a "normal" family story and

get over former relationships. Of course single parenting can result from several different situations (pregnancy out of wedlock, death of one's spouse, divorce). But there always is a grieving period, and a need to let go emotionally of the other parent.

3. They can accept the past and come to terms with it. The past isn't forgotten. The deceased spouse is still missed, or the divorced spouse is still a source of anger.

4. They make time for themselves:
☐ Have friends and activities that *don't* involve the kids.
☐ Keep spiritually, mentally and physically fit.
☐ Simplify life. They don't try to do it all. They learn to say no. They eliminate unnecessary stresses. They also learn appropriate ways to deal with anger.

5. They reach out for help when needed:
☐ Avoid getting into serious financial difficulty.
☐ Work hard to prevent ex-spouses from controlling their lives.

6. They handle children appropriately:
☐ Don't make children their whole life.
☐ Allow kids to be kids. They recognize age-appropriate behavior.
☐ Let children know that they count, and that they can count on the parent. They set aside positive time to be with their kids.
☐ Are able to hear and accept the children's feelings . . . and these are often very negative (anger, guilt, depression).
☐ Continue to set limits.

7. They have come to terms with guilt:
☐ Know the difference between legitimate guilt (breaking God's standards) and illegitimate guilt (going against the "shoulds" and "oughts" learned in childhood that don't square with God's laws). They know how to ask, *What part of this is actually my fault?*
☐ Take action if guilt is legitimate, seeking forgiveness and restitution.

Family life together. Now let's put all the pieces together as all the characters come in contact with each other and begin to relate to one another. Here are the elements that make up a well-written family story.

1. Families protect and love us. In protecting us, parents keep us safe. In loving us, parents make us feel whole and worthwhile. In both activities parents teach us to trust. The experiences of love in our families are stored away for future use. We learn how to love, whom to love and how to be lovable just by growing up in our families and experiencing the love that is there.

Well-written family stories

□ are written by two partners who love each other. This was discussed above in the section on healthy couples.

□ include affection demonstrated to all their members. Sibling rivalry tends to develop when children in the family perceive that love is distributed unequally (it can be argued whether the perception is valid or not).

□ do not include cliques. Some of the most destructive cliques or coalitions I have seen involve mother-son and father-daughter coalitions. I've also seen cross-generational coalitions between grandparents and grandchildren that have been extremely destructive to other family members.

□ are marked by fun enjoyed together and apart. Traditions are built within these families, and thus memories are made. Remember, quality time is always couched in quantity time.

□ use humor positively. Family members are not the butt of well-aimed sarcasm or ridicule. Family members laugh with each other, not at each other.

2. Families define us. They tell us who we are. They mold the character each of us will be in our unfolding stories and give us the roles we will play in those stories.

These well-written family stories

□ maintain clear boundaries that are neither too close or too distant. Boundaries mark limits. They also protect priorities. Boundaries mark off each individual in the family. Each is unique with his or her own thoughts, feelings and actions. Privacy is respected, which includes external privacy (people don't burst in and out of each other's rooms or the bathroom when others are there) and internal privacy (people can keep certain thoughts to themselves and are encouraged to think for themselves).

☐ allow parents to reserve certain issues for themselves. Everyone else in the family knows there's a special bond between Mom and Dad that others aren't allowed to participate in.

3. Families model for us what society is all about. A family can be seen as an entire society between four walls.

In the family legal system there is a hierarchy (parents are in charge), limits and guidelines are set, and penalties are exacted. As a result, families teach us how to deal with authority, to set right what is wrong and to choose among options.

In well-written families, people can forgive each other. This starts with Dad. (Many children have said to me over the years, "He never admits he's wrong.") Everyone in the family understands the steps that lead to reconciliation. When our children were young, we taught them to ask forgiveness when they had wronged someone. We also taught them to grant forgiveness when they were the ones wronged.

Then there's the family economic system, where people learn how to earn money, how to invest it, how to share it with those less fortunate and in general how to take responsibility for their own well-being. Children learn how to spend, how to save, how to delay needs. They also learn values—what's really important in life.

4. Families offer a sense of continuity linking past stories with future stories. As Dolores Curran writes in her book on healthy families, "The family honors its elders and welcomes its babies."[14] In well-written family stories we're taught where we've come from, giving us a sense of place in history. In many ways the story also points us toward the future, showing us where we are going. In these families, members realize they are not alone. They are not stranded in time.

The family treasures its legends ("Uncle Max was a no-good until Aunt Tillie found him, married him and cleaned him up") and characters ("Your great-granddaddy hid in the hayloft for four years so he wouldn't be conscripted into the Confederate Army"). In telling and retelling the stories, the family learns what it is to be part of an ongoing family story.

The well-written story is a "museum of memories," as Edith Schaeffer says.[15] Traditions and celebrations are relished and repeated as central events in the ongoing life of the family. Traditions give our life stability, predictability and meaning.

5. From families we learn about ourselves as individuals and as parts of networks of relationships. Thus we learn how to interact with others, how to express ourselves and listen, how to be sensitive to other people's needs and how to be tolerant of other people's lives. As a result we learn how to get along with each other in various situations.

Characters in these well-written family stories

□ have a sense of wonderment about each individual. Diversity is celebrated. As a result, everyone feels loved and appreciated for who they are. Children aren't constantly struggling to meet parental expectations that don't correlate with who the child actually is. Each member joins in the chorus of praise for every other member. This, of course, is led by parents who first feel good about themselves.

□ disagree agreeably. They know how to fight *and* they know how to make up. Two extremes are found in poorly written families. Conflict is out of control, always verbally destructive, sometimes physically so; or the family is so terrified of conflict that no one ever disagrees. Submerged conflict is in many ways just as dangerous as overt conflict. Well-written family stories have many disagreements, but these are managed well.

□ have a support network. These families can reach beyond themselves for help and support. There's extended family ready to be helpful, along with church connections, friends in the community and others to whom the family can turn in times of crisis.

6. Families teach us what feelings and emotions are, and how to express these. Families laugh and cry. Families are afraid. Families are exhilarated. People come and go. There are traditions and celebrations. People please and offend, compliment and ridicule. In all these experiences, emotions are generated and expressed.

In well-written stories, characters communicate clearly and congruently. There are no secrets or coalitions. Individual feelings and independent thinking are encouraged (Eph 4:15).

7. Families teach us what is true (Deut 4:9; 6:6-7). A family constructs reality for its members, demonstrating by word and deed what is important, what is to be valued, what is true and false, what is the nature of the world around us.

Faith for the well-written family is fundamental to its existence and ongoing functioning. Spiritual values are incorporated into all aspects of family life. Faith is discussed and demonstrated in positive and meaningful ways.

Well-written family stories are flexible, changing and adapting to differing situations as the family story develops over time, while maintaining a core of unchanging ingredients (values, traditions, beliefs).

8. Families do not exist for themselves alone. They reach beyond themselves with a mission (a vocation) in mind. I've known families that were dedicated to inner-city work, soup kitchens or nursing homes. These families had chosen an area of ministry where every family member, no matter how young or old, could participate and serve.

The well-written family is generous, sharing with others from the resources it has been given. The well-written family is also hospitable, welcoming outsiders into its home.

9. Families help us grow to maturity and then permit us to leave to begin writing our own family stories. From an early age, parents realize that their job is to work themselves out of a job, so responsibilities are turned over to the children as they are able to assume various tasks.

Obviously there is no family story that includes all of these elements. However, the above list gives us a baseline from which we can consider our own family stories, with an eye toward strengthening areas that are deficient and changing situations that need alteration.

2
A Look at the Story's Authors

Why don't you talk? Can't you defend yourself?"
Mary Simmons faced her husband Bill. His eyes would not look in
her direction. Her husband of over twenty-eight years continued to
stare blankly at the floor as if frozen, afraid to move, afraid to speak.
Mary slumped back in her chair, defeated.

"Why don't you both take a deep breath for a moment?" I decided
to break into the conversation and rescue them for the time being,
realizing that we weren't getting anywhere. "Let's take our time and
unpack this thing and see what's brought you to this place."

Mary and Bill had driven up from the Shenandoah to my northern
Virginia office in an attempt to figure out what was happening in their
family. They wanted to be as far away from their small town as was
practical. Now I was going to attempt to find out how their family
story had been written, and what changes needed to be made.

Mary Simmons came from a very destructive, confrontational
family. In her family story, confrontation was an accepted way of life.
In some ways it was the only means to show affection. Whenever any
issue was brought up by one family member, the person introducing
the issue was challenged by one or more other family members. "If
you didn't challenge the person with the issue," Mary explained in my

office, "you showed that person that you really didn't care." As a result of this early training, most of her thinking took place externally, in dialogue with others.

But of course there was also a sinister side to her parents' style, especially her father's. Confrontation had slipped over into criticism. Discipline strayed into abuse. And criticism had been his way of motivating Mary and her siblings. "You're not pretty enough. You didn't do well in school. You don't eat properly" sounded throughout the house as she was growing up. Mary felt chronically incompetent, as if nothing she did was ever quite enough to bring affirmation.

Bill came from a quiet, physically demonstrative family. A critical part of his family story was a lack of disagreement. " 'Never disagree, and always hug,' Mom would say," Bill explained. All conflict in this family was submerged. So much of his thinking took place in solitude, where he often retreated to contemplate and strategize his actions.

Acceptance and rejection were primary themes running through this family's story. And Bill never felt secure in the fact that he was acceptable and lovable. Bill became a slave of routine, hoping that if he didn't "make waves" and if he followed all instructions to the letter, he would ultimately be acceptable.

But for now I just stared at them, my mind racing, wondering how best to intervene, what to say to put these two people back on track and begin the process of unfolding their story, to see where the plot had gone wrong. How had they managed to write a story that was now causing both of them so much pain?

Looking Back at Your Story

Perhaps you have never had the privilege of attempting to author your own family story with a spouse—though you inevitably write your personal story each day. This chapter will help you understand how your parents or caregivers wrote the family story that formed you. It will lead you into insights into what happened before and what is happening now.

Or perhaps you, like me, are well along in the writing of your own family story. You've created a character or two (your kids, that is) and are currently involved with your spouse in some particular chapter in your life story. This chapter should give you insights into the way your parents authored their family story, and it will assist you in your writing now that you have the liberty to create your own story.

The Primary Authors Go to Work

Parents are the primary writers of a family story. The family stories from which they emerged give the primary material for each spouse to begin writing. However, because there are usually two writers—husband and wife—working simultaneously on the family story project, many conflicts and compromises must be negotiated.

So your parents, or perhaps your primary caregivers (people who actually raised you but were not birth or adoptive parents), were the people who authored the family story and started writing your personal story as well. Let's look at the various standard chapters (these chapters vary in combined family stories) to see how the story starts to unfold.

Chapter 1: The Primary Authors Meet and Court

Actually, before our authors (boyfriend and girlfriend) meet and become serious about each other, several important foundational story lines must be established. These story lines involve your personal story and your family-of-origin story. Your personal story and your family story are different, though there is a great deal of overlap, each affecting the other. In this chapter our emphasis will be on the development of the family story. The next chapter will focus on the personal story development.

Let's follow Mary as she journeys toward Bill and finally becomes his wife. Mary and Bill emerge from two different families where different family stories were unfolding.

Mary was born into the Sideropoulous family, so she was a part of the Sideropoulous family story. The present Sideropoulous family story was actually the continuation of a story that had been unfolding through the generations, both in Greece and in America. The family story could be traced back through many generations. But for our purposes, surveying the story through three or four generations back will suffice. If Mary had taken the time to do a little research and knew what she was looking for, she would have found a consistent story line emerging in her family, a story line with familiar themes emerging in generation after generation.

Family stories are interesting when viewed over generations. What emerges is a pattern in which story lines that are not appropriately resolved in one generation are passed on into the next generation to be worked on. If unsuccessfully dealt with in the succeeding generation, the story line again is passed on (the sins of the parents visited on the third and fourth generation—see Ex 20:5). In this way we perpetuate the past. We choose people and form relationships that are familiar to us, even when they may be toxic to us.

As you continue reading, begin to think about the themes that have been resident in your family down through the generations. You may want to begin a diagram, or "genogram," of your family over several generations. Using squares for males and circles for females, diagram your family as I have diagrammed the Simmons family in figure 2. If you begin a genogram now, you can use it throughout the book.

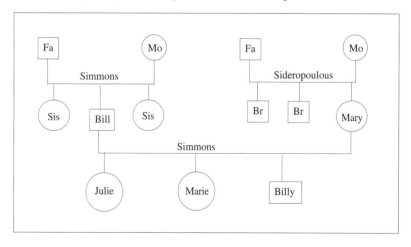

Figure 2. Genogram of the Simmons family

As Mary grew up, her personal story was slowly written even as the Sideropoulous family story continued to unfold around her. Mary's personal story was greatly influenced by the Sideropoulous family story line that had unfolded for many years. This family story had cherished achievement, and various relatives in the past had risen to positions of prominence in industry and the military. But women in this family were not valued as were the men, and Mary felt an underlying theme of dissatisfaction and criticism of her performance, though she worked hard and did well in all she attempted. Such would be Mary's legacy as her personal story unfolded.

Mary got pregnant out of wedlock at age sixteen, as had her mother and grandmother before her. She had given up the baby for adoption long before she met Bill Simmons. The issue underlying this behavior had been a gnawing sense of inadequacy on the part of each of the women in the Sideropoulous family. To "prove" adequacy, each had gotten pregnant. ("See, I have made a baby. I can create something meaningful. I can make something of my life.") Of course, not only had this *not* solved the issue of inadequacy, it had *increased* the sense of inadequacy—an issue that was passed on in each case to a daughter, who repeated the cycle.

A separate personal story must include a firmly established identity (self) before one begins one's search for a lifelong mate. Mary's identity brought order and meaning to her existence. To form a personal story, we must overcome personal inadequacies, learn to associate with peers, launch a career and find a place in the adult world.

For us as young adults to reach this time of life successfully, our personal story needs to have developed apart from our family story (the next chapter will discuss the particulars of this). To have written a successful personal story to this point, a story that allows us to launch off into the world, we must have included several key ingredients:

☐ Responsibility. I can take responsibility for myself and my actions. I am not in a reactive, victim position, feeling as though everyone and everything is working against me.

☐ Autonomy. I am able to take action alone. I can take responsibility to be the primary writer of my personal story.

☐ Perseverance. I have "stick-to-itiveness," the ability to follow through on projects begun.

☐ Initiative. I can seize the initiative and be active, not eternally passive.

☐ Interdependence. I can get along with and draw from the resources of others.

The less we have grown away from our own family story as we shape our personal story, the more anxiety we will experience about being on our own and assuming responsibility for ourselves. Some people deal with this by never leaving their family. Others seem to have grown up, moved out on their own and begun writing their own stories; but the charade is betrayed as their anxiety continues to mount every time they attempt to act responsibly apart from parents.

Bill and Mary Simmons have difficulties in their family stories. In spite of this, both developed personal stories that are reasonably well written. Now they are ready for the next step in their story. These young people are reasonably well established as adults, and they both contain within their minds a storehouse of unmet needs, character sketches and story lines from which they will draw as they seek a spouse who will (1) help to cowrite a new family story, (2) serve as a character in the ongoing family story as it is written and (3) assist the spouse in the writing of his or her personal story. They've both been exposed to the unfolding stories of their parents' marriages. They've experienced numerous other male-female story lines. They've examined closely members of the opposite sex. They've been coached culturally in how to act their own parts as male/husband and female/wife. And they have a reasonable understanding of biblical mandates for marriage.

All of this might sound complicated. Don't two people just meet, like what they see in each other and marry? Having talked to hundreds upon hundreds of couples, I don't think so. These two people who are meeting each other are actually already involved as characters in two distinct family stories that are unfolding. Each person will select another person (potential spouse) who will be more or less ideal as a cowriter and as a character (the writers will step into the drama they are writing and help unfold the plot).

So Bill and Mary meet. Both just happen to be in the public library one Saturday morning, browsing in the biography section. They're struck with each other from the start (they'll tell this story over and over again to friends in the coming years). The real electricity in the attraction between the two involves the unfinished story line from each person's past.

In the personal story Bill continues to write, he longs for acceptance, feeling down deep that this is a void in his life, that he is somehow defective and incomplete because his parents never said, "Bill, we think you're a good person. This is what we like about you." He had gone to college, excelled in accounting, graduated and become a CPA, but had never had the satisfaction of knowing he was acceptable.

Enter Mary, who in many ways reminds him of his physically close, emotionally distant parents. But Mary also embodies qualities that Bill doesn't. Mary likes to keep things up front and "on the table." She's alive and borders on irreverent. She's bouncy, spontaneous, impulsive. Growing up, Mary seemed to be into everything—cheerleading, writing, community service, church work. She merrily bounced from project to project.

Though sweet, humorous and attractive, Mary never seems able to validate any of Bill's talents or abilities. But this is ignored as the two focus on what they like about each other and what they have in common.

Mary is attracted to Bill because he is quiet and steady. He starts a project and finishes it, sticking closely to routine. His consistency is a comfort to her, because she can predict what he will do, and he always does it. Ignored by Mary is Bill's tendency to overlook her accomplishments, and even to be somewhat intimidated by her competencies.

This is a simplification, of course, for as we come to marriage, the storehouses in our minds virtually brim with stories, story remnants, well-formed characters and character fragments. In fact, another important factor in choosing a spouse has to do with parts of myself (for example, the spontaneous part, the methodical part) that were denied to me and locked away, but remain loaded with emotional energy. (This will be taken up in chapter three, when I talk about the formation of character.) Both Bill and Mary will dip into their storehouses to begin writing the new story of their family.

Mary and Bill have been attracted to each other because (1) each exhibit characteristics that the other lacks (Mary's outgoing spontaneity, Bill's quiet steadiness and eye to routine) and (2) each didn't get something emotionally important in childhood and now looks to the other to supply it—though they also realize the other's inability to provide it (Bill seeks a sense of acceptance, Mary seeks a sense of competence).

So Mary and Bill behold each other. Each screens his or her perceptions of the other through a filter made up largely of the "ideal mate" image in his or her own mind's storehouse (see figure 3). This ideal mate will be one who will heal the most prominent childhood wounds each has suffered. Because all images coming to Bill and

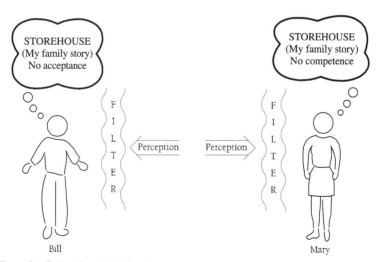

Figure 3. Seeing the potential mate

Mary are filtered, perceptions are altered. Neither is able to see the other clearly. But they know they will just be "perfect" for each other, so they decide to marry.

Emotionally, this couple is at a point in their mutual story that I call *stuck*. They're bonding intensely with each other. Passions run high. Both perceive a great deal of nurture from the other. There are few demands from either person to change. "I just want to do and be whatever you want" is the story line that is repeated by both. Differences between the two are minimized ("We seem to share everything"). And certainly, the issues that will later haunt them—the unmet childhood needs, the ways in which each is different from the other—are all ignored.

Exercise. Set the book aside for a moment and consider the following questions. First answer the questions for your parents' courtship (if you don't know the answers, ask your parents or people who knew them when they were young). Then, if you're married or now courting, answer for your relationship. As with all the exercises, either write the answers in your journal or discuss them with a small group.

1. Think of your personal story (or that of each of your parents) for a moment. What comes to mind as the central themes of your life? (For example, "I was lonely a lot"; or, "I entertained everyone in the family.") Write a list of the themes of your story that were important to you.

2. Make a list of the key characteristics of your parents or caregivers, both positive and negative. Circle those characteristics that were the most prominent in your development.

3. How did you meet your future spouse? Which of you initiated the dating? How would you describe the first date? What was it about your mate that made you want to date him or her again?

4. What traits, behaviors and characteristics about your mate did you find most attractive back then? Which did you dislike? How did you deal with the negative traits?

5. How did your physical relationship develop? Was it basically positive or negative?

6. Were your parents supportive of the relationship? Any reserva-
tions? What were your friends' reactions to your relationship?
   7. How was the decision to marry first considered? Who proposed?
Were there special circumstances (death of parent, illness or the like)?
How long was the engagement, and did it progress smoothly?

Chapter 2: The Primary Authors Get Married

Mary, being the action-oriented, impulsive person that she was, urged
a quick courtship and marriage. Bill had already learned to go along
with her, having felt her critical barbs once or twice. So Mary and Bill
picked a sunny afternoon in late June, reserved a church and a banquet
hall, found a preacher and got married.

One day early in their marriage, Mary launched into a passionate
statement about the Cold War. (Based on her family story, she was
showing how much she cared, plus she liked to think out loud to
organize her thoughts.) Bill, somewhat aghast, rushed to hug her and
tame the onslaught (returning his sense of care by defusing the
disagreement). Now it was Mary's turn to be disoriented.

"What are you doing, you nincompoop! Why are you such a jerk
all the time?" Mary attacked, wiggling out of Bill's grasp. Deep down,
Mary was sure that criticism would motivate her new husband. But
Bill stared blankly, completely stunned and unable to speak, his mind
flooded with emotions he could not handle. Criticism was no motivator to him. It scared him and made him feel unacceptable.

But the more Bill retreated from her, the more Mary felt unaffirmed
and incompetent. She pursued Bill, only making him withdraw faster.
Soon Bill and Mary retreated to safe areas of the house, Mary to the
kitchen, Bill to his workbench.

Mary and Bill typify the average married couple. The average
woman is very willing to plunge into the conflicts that periodically
arise in even the healthiest of marriages. Women learn at an early age
that talking brings resolution. Men, on the other hand, tend to fear
these discussions, realizing that they are prone to becoming emotionally overwhelmed at lower levels of distress. (Of course some women

have the same response; you may recall that it was from his mother that Bill learned to avoid conflict.) Bill, like the majority of men, stonewalls his wife in an attempt to defuse the mounting distress. To his dismay, this strategy not only doesn't defuse the situation but actually ignites it further, as Mary feels ignored and responds with an attack.

When we leave our parents to marry, we actually leave the two people who have been the primary authors not only of the family story but of our own personal story as well. When we take a spouse, we acquire an author who will assist us in writing a new family story, and who will also assist to a greater or lesser degree (depending on how much each individual assumes responsibility for his own story) with the writing of our personal stories.

Mary's parents had written her personal story to include a sense of inadequacy. Bill continued writing this theme for Mary, though she had unconsciously hoped he would rewrite this segment to make her feel adequate. At the same time, Mary picked up where Bill's parents left off in the writing of his character as unacceptable and not worthy of endorsement, though he had hoped she would write in a sense of acceptability for him.

Simultaneous with the continued writing of their personal stories, the couple continued to forge their new family story. Prominent in this story was Mary's confronting Bill whenever he attempted to raise an issue and criticizing him when she wanted him to act. Bill slowly learned to become more passive and withdrawn when he was at home around Mary (a strategy from his personal story, one he had employed when he was a teenager with his parents). He would rarely raise an issue, any issue, with Mary.

Bill's withdrawal frightened Mary, who felt as though he was showing her to be defective and inadequate. So the more he withdrew, the more she criticized. And so whenever he even thought of discussing anything of importance with her, his stomach would tense up.

Mary gradually began to feel that Bill didn't really love her. He never confronted her (never showed he cared). In fact, she sensed his uneasiness whenever he was around her. They were at this point when they came to see me for counseling.

As you were born (or adopted) into your family and began to observe your parents' unfolding story, a wide range of attitudes and behaviors slowly took shape deep inside of you, attitudes that would greatly affect the way you later would write your own family story:

☐ how you viewed the opposite sex
☐ the role of touching in your life (did you like to touch and be touched?)
☐ whether or not you expressed your thoughts and feelings
☐ how you solved problems
☐ how you would rear your own children
☐ how you would relate to in-laws
☐ how money would be handled
☐ how issues of power and control would be handled (who would lead and follow)
☐ how physical and emotional boundaries between people would be delineated and maintained

You probably didn't realize that many of these key attitudes and practices had been resident in your family story for generations. Each of these attitudes and experiences, as you grew, was neatly tucked away in your storehouse, to be plucked out later and used in your own story development.

As you dated, you checked potential mates against the image that had slowly formed in your storehouse as to what the ideal mate would be like—how he or she would act, talk, behave in myriad situations. *This is the character who will enter my story, and be not only be a character in my ongoing story but a cowriter with me as together we set out to write a new family story.*

Unfortunately, this ideal-mate template contained many contradictions and partial images that made the process something other than exact. But in spite of the contradictions, a couple manages to come together and marry. Many differences, contradictions and possible story difficulties remained in the dark because the couple was still in the "stuck" phase emotionally, thus minimizing any potential roadblocks while emphasizing the positive about each other and the relationship.

As two people marry, they must reorganize all the material from their original family stories and fuse it into the new family story they will now write. The individual stories are also used to form the new family story, while they are also altered and adjusted for each partner.

Each spouse "spreads out" his expectations of how the story should be written—all his or her perspectives on life, love, intimacy, sex and so on. In some areas the couple is more intense than in others. These areas—the emotional mine fields that blow up periodically for all couples—are the areas we've already seen in the lives of Bill and Mary. Mary fears the message "you're incompetent"; Bill fears the message "you're not acceptable."

Critical to the unfolding marital story are not only the emotional issues in each partner's storehouse but also the circumstances that surrounded the decision to marry. Did one or both partners marry to escape an intolerable home situation? Did parents of both partners support the union, or was there tension and lack of consent?

Therefore the first awkward sentences of the family story that took shape between Bill and Mary would later have profound effects on the children who had not yet been born to them.

Exercise. Lay the book aside again and do the following.

1. Lay out your personal story theme list from the exercise above. If your spouse hasn't done so already, have your spouse do a similar list of his or her personal story, and lay this beside your list.

2. Note similarities and differences in the two personal stories.

3. Circle in red ink those themes in both of the stories where conflict arose. (For example, "I was alone. Now I like to be by myself, and this causes friction with my spouse.")

4. See if you can identify for yourself the key emotional issue that "hooks" you and gets you very intense emotionally (for example, lack of acceptance; or a feeling of being out of control; or incompetence).

Chapter 3: The Children Come

"Hello, Mom, I've got great news." Mary brimmed with excitement as she squeezed the telephone receiver and spoke with her usual rapid-fire delivery. "I'm pregnant!" Mary and Bill had been married now for three years. They had started trying to have a baby for only a few months when the results of the pregnancy test were conclusive.

"Mary, that's wonderful!" her mother exulted. "That will make me a grandmother for the first time! Is everything all right with you, you know, with the baby and all?"

"Yes, Mother, just fine. You don't have to mother me now."

As the family story continues to unfold, our author couple adds a new important chapter: a child is born to them. At this point in the story, there is a switch from "each other" to "the three of us." Instantly subplots are created:

What is the role of the newly created grandparents? Have both these "children" adequately withdrawn from their family of origin stories, or does one or the other or both continue to play key roles in those old stories? For Bill and Mary, differences in family traditions came strongly into play at this point. Mary's parents wanted the new little daughter christened in the Greek Orthodox Church. Bill's parents felt just as strongly that the child should receive a Presbyterian baptism. Though Bill and Mary had disagreed about the role of parents in their lives, they had successfully kept the disagreements under control until this issue emerged.

Are initial marriage promises still honored? A new life adds pressure to the couple now become three. In the face of not getting as much from the partner as before, the promise must sustain them.

After a child is born, love must, more than ever, focus on the other and his or her needs rather than on the self and its needs. Many new fathers feel left out of their wife's love, sensing competition from the new infant. Wives often find that their husbands pull away emotionally, devoting more and more time to climbing career ladders or developing hobbies away from home.

Intimacy and passion may both be rocky and need to be readjusted and worked at intentionally so that the couple does not drift apart.

Expectations must be renegotiated with changing roles. New

young mothers assume heavy parenting obligations, even when they are working outside the home. These wives expect husbands to help out with parenting.

For the first time in their marriage, Mary was in a needy position, requiring nurture from Bill. Could he make the shift? Now Mary and Bill had new roles as parents. Also they faced a great need to maintain the boundary around themselves as a couple, in the face of demands from a new family member.

James M. Herzog conducted a retrospective study of 103 first-time fathers of premature babies. What he found can be simply summarized: the greater the new father's hunger for his own father (due to his father's uninvolvement with him when he was growing up), the less able he is to participate successfully in expectant fatherhood.[1] Generalizing to both husband and wife, we can also say that if either of them has not sorted out the conflicts he or she had with his or her own parents, those conflicts more than likely will be recapitulated when they become parents themselves.

We saw this motif first in the marriage chapter. When a couple gets married, unfinished business from chapters in our family of origin story emerges and is played out again in the present. So it is when a child is born, more unfinished business in the parents' stories is resurrected and reinstituted.

Each couple, as children are conceived, are in the midst of a particular story. You may have been conceived before your parents were married. Perhaps they never married, and your birth was not welcomed. Your birth may have been completely disruptive to your mother's story, and she may have made you aware of this all your life. One woman who had come to America from a Third World country related to me how her parents, when she was very young, left her out in the elements, hoping she would die. She was the second of two sisters and was completely unwanted in her family story.

Perhaps you were born following the death of a cherished relative (say a brother or a grandfather), and you were expected to pick up the fragments of that person's story and live out his character in your own life. Or possibly you were conceived to save your parents' marriage, so that you grew up under pressure to be the mediator between your parents. Or your parents were extremely happy in their marital story and planned to have you. Your birth may have been a symbol to them of their love and devotion to each other.

As several children are introduced into the family, these siblings form each child's first peer group. The children learn to support each other, to attack, scapegoat, manipulate, support, enjoy and generally learn from each other. This is the crucial context in which all of us learn to compete, to cooperate and to negotiate. We learn to achieve recognition, to make friends, to deal with enemies. We learn how to be different and how to be similar. We look at our brothers and sisters, compare our lot with theirs and begin to form a picture of the world as basically just or unjust. We then look at ourselves and decide that we are either generally worthwhile or not good enough.

The couple, beginning to flex their parental muscles, exhibit different styles as they prepare to raise their new offspring. Some parents become very authoritarian. These parents do not want to relinquish any power as the child is growing up. Independence is threatening, and they will clamp down all the harder when they sense that their child is beginning to manifest even the smallest degree of autonomy. Children growing up in these family stories tend to be dependent, submissive and insecure and have difficulty with creativity.

Other parents turn out to be quite permissive. They find it very difficult to set any boundaries for their children. Rather than being strong and directive, these parents continually vacillate. The child is never quite sure from day to day what is expected and what the family standards are. Children growing up in these families tend to have low levels of self-reliance and self-control and tend not to want to go out and explore new worlds.

The third type of parents are authoritative. These parents take a firm stand and present clear boundaries to their children, but they tend not to jump in and solve all their children's problems (as the authoritarian parent would). They gently but firmly challenge their child to find solutions to problems herself, to make mistakes and to profit from those mistakes. Children raised in this atmosphere (provided that there is a great deal of love and acceptance mixed in) tend to be independent, happy, self-starting and able to take on new challenges.

Exercise. Think about each of your parents for a moment. If you want, close your eyes and picture each in your mind. Begin with your father (you may choose stepfather or father surrogate if you like). Think of one or two adjectives that best describe his overall parenting style as you understood it as a child—for example, doting, seductive, warm, distant, affirming, supportive, demanding, weak, jovial.

Write a brief profile of your father in your journal. Then, think of how you responded to your father and his parenting style. For example:

☐ "I always tried to get his attention."

☐ "I wanted to please him."

☐ "I tried to get away from him."

Now go through the same process, this time thinking of your mother. Write down her characteristics and then the way that you responded to her. Your journal entry may then look something like this:

FATHER

Characteristics	*Responses*
Distant	I constantly tried to get his attention.

MOTHER

Characteristics	*Responses*
Affirming	I felt very much accepted and loved.

It is at this time in a marriage that emotionally the couple, who have been stuck together in high passion, begin to become *unstuck* (or, more usually, one of the partners begins to "unstick" emotionally). Each partner begins to reestablish his or her own boundaries, pursue his and her own interests again and reconnect with his or her individual story.

There is a shift toward internally defining each partner's sense of self with independent thoughts, feelings and needs.

Unfortunately, as one partner begins the process of becoming unstuck, the other partner may see this as a threat to the relationship and, in a panic, go to extreme means to reestablish the old sense of emotional stuckness. When this is unsuccessful, there is a grief process over the loss of the intense times the couple experienced together.

The basic dilemma during this story chapter becomes, How do I become aware of my wants and of your wants, and how do I strike a balance between our different wants and needs? How can I shift roles from being a spouse to being a spouse *and* a parent? And how can I keep spouse, parent, employee, parishioner, soccer coach, scout leader and so on in the proper balance as these stories unfold around me?

Exercise. Take out your journal, or discuss with your small group the following questions.

1. What do you think your mother's reaction was when she saw you for the first time after your birth? your father's reaction?

2. Were your parents glad that you were a girl? boy?

3. What was your first memory of your family? Does this memory bring pleasant or unpleasant feelings?

4. What circumstances, beliefs and values do you think played a part in your parents' decision to have the number of children they had? What circumstances played into the decision to have you?

5. What do you think your siblings' reactions were when you were born? What was your reaction when they were born?

Alternative: Draw a picture of your family, when you were young, doing something together. Show your picture to your spouse or a close friend and discuss what's taking place.

Chapter 4: The Children Go Off to School

Mary and Bill watched as their first child, Julie, climbed aboard the school bus and headed for her first day of kindergarten. They'd already taken pictures, helped in clothing selection and adornment, and given the pep talk about how to act.

At this time the family story takes a dramatic twist, a twist that many parent/writers are not aware of. For it is as the children begin to go off to school that several important themes begin to unfold.

First, the child who is going off to school is less dependent on the parents. A child's friends begin to exert an influence that will have powerful ramifications as the child's story continues to unfold. At the same time, outside influences are brought to bear on family.

Second, demands of the family and demands of the career make intimacy tougher to maintain. As Bill and Mary saw the last of their children off to school, Mary decided that it was time to return to work. This was a jarring announcement to Bill, who always envisioned himself as the breadwinner *(I am competent),* with Mary firmly fixed at home caring for the children.

Emotionally, there often develops between the couple what I call the *I-ness* (or independence) stage. The spouses often find themselves participating in activities and relationships away from the other, concentrating more on their personal stories than on the family story. Unfortunately, for many couples the paths diverge never again to reconnect. Others, after a time of personal story development, reconnect with each other and begin again to concentrate on the writing of the family story.

Exercise. Again take out your journal. Write the answers to these questions and/or discuss with your group.

1. When you first left home for school in your family of origin, what significant events were taking place in your family (moving, job loss, other)? How did these experiences affect your first experience of school?

2. As you met new friends, were these people welcomed into your home? Did you find it easy or difficult to make new friends? Were you encouraged or discouraged in your quest for friends?

3. During this time, did your parents seem more distant from each other? What did each of your parents do with their spare time? Did they spend any time together doing things each enjoyed?

If you are currently in this chapter with your children or have traversed it, go back and answer the questions now in relation to your present family story.

Chapter 5: The Couple Reaches Midlife
Bill and Mary both admit that they never really realized how difficult life could be until their story reached the chapter commonly titled "midlife." It wasn't just the subplot of Mary's father dying and her mother coming to live with the family. That just added some spice to a story that was already extremely complicated.

The children were now growing into their teen years and reaching toward independence. This proved to be extremely painful for Mary, who had always wanted a close family in which everyone would be willing to take part in lots of shared activities. Instead the kids wanted to be off with friends doing their own activities. It was hard for Mary even to get the family together for a meal during the week.

Mary was surprised as she entered menopause that she felt a sense of loss, the loss of the ability to have children. Not that she wanted more—that thought was absurd. But she missed the capacity to have more, as if part of her womanhood was gone. Accompanying this was a fear that now she was sexless and because of this was in danger of losing Bill to another, younger woman.

For Bill there came the questions of adequacy, fulfillment and direction. Added to this was the nagging question he hadn't posed since adolescence: *Who am I?* His stomach was starting to bulge over his belt. His hair was thinning. He couldn't play on the church softball team any longer, at least at the level he desired. And to top it off, Bill felt stuck in his concrete company. Successful though he had been, now he was tired of making sure concrete showed up at construction sites when it was supposed to.

It was at this point that Bill felt called to the ministry. He was surprised that Mary was so supportive. He sold his business, and with that money invested, he was able to take the family to a new town and enter seminary. After three years he found himself the assistant pastor in a large suburban church. Several years after that he was back in the Shenandoah with his own church.

Back when Bill was stumbling around attempting to refocus his life, he and Mary both found the need to renegotiate their expectations and roles. This was made doubly hard because of the drift that had taken place between the two over the years. Intimacy and passion had waned in recent years, as the two had learned to carve out their personal stories with minimal involvement from the other.

Exercise. Again, take out your journal, and write out the answers to the following questions.

1. In your family-of-origin story, was there a particular time when you became aware that your parents were struggling with what we commonly call midlife issues? What was happening in your parents' lives? How old were you? How did this affect your life?

2. If you are currently struggling with these issues in your own marriage, what is your particular experience of the struggle? What are the issues between you and your spouse as you currently understand them?

Chapter 6: The Couple Has an Empty Nest

"What do we do with each other?" Mary asked Bill as the two watched their youngest son climb aboard a plane and fly off to college. For well over twenty years Bill and Mary had focused much of their attention on their children—school events, church outings, sports, vacations. The house was never empty. Bill and Mary had welcomed their kids' friends in at any time. "It's an open-door policy here." Now that was all gone. Bill and Mary were entering a new chapter in their family story, a chapter commonly titled "the empty nest."

During this chapter several new challenges arise. Can we effectively let our children go? For some couples this is not so easy. Children, for these couples, not only have been the primary focus of their lives but have served as buffers between the couple to deflect conflict. For these couples, to let the last of the children go would be to court disaster.

The second major issue in this chapter is whether the couple can deal with each other effectively. For most successful couples, the new emotional phase entered can be called *we-ness* (or unity). Now that both have established their own identity, each can look to the other again for intimacy and emotional support. Ideally each partner has found satisfaction in his or her own life and now can develop a deep, mutually satisfying bond. With such a bond would come the reemergence of vulnerability. A balance between *I* and *us* would also be more firmly established. Then would come the capacity to respond more consistently to each other's needs.

Unfortunately, for some the story takes a tragic turn. The couple is unable to pull back together and focus primary attention on each other. Some couples pull apart in divorce, startling friends and family after years of married life. Others, though still legally married, focus attention on their own personal stories and have little to do with their partner.

Exercise. Write or discuss your answers to the following.

1. What was your leaving home like? Did your parents have an easy time saying goodby, or was there turmoil associated with this?

2. After you left home, were you able to focus primarily on your new pursuits (college or job), or were you constantly distracted by matters back home?

3. Did you in any way feel responsible for your parents' well-being?

4. After all of the children in your family of origin had left home, how would you rate your parents' marriage: excellent? good? fair? poor? On what do you base your rating?

Chapter 7: Retirement

Bill and Mary had not reached retirement age yet, but they had thought about it and planned for it for some time and they had watched as both sets of their parents had retired. Mary's parents had seemed to make the transition without difficulty. They continued to live in their own home, travel, visit their children and grandchildren, and generally live productively until Mary's father died, at which time it was decided that the best thing to do was to have Mary's mother come and live with Bill and Mary.

Bill's parents had a rocky transition. Though they had stayed together over the years, their relationship had never been close. Their relationship seemed year by year to grow more strained and distant. After retirement Bill's father lapsed further into alcoholism. His mother busied herself with volunteer work outside the home. Both died in their early seventies, within months of each other.

As the family story finally winds down, the couple faces retirement and the eventual death of a spouse. The story takes on new twists as the couple is now home together, usually with a minimum of outside interferences. Each spouse has had to learn new roles in relation to the other, the larger family and the outside community. In Western societies aging usually brings a loss of status in the community. Illness brings new incapacitation and possible role reversals, so that a spouse who has always been a giver now must be a receiver. Expectations need to be reassessed. Finally comes the death of a spouse, and the attendant grieving process.

As people reach this chapter and look back over the unfolding story of their lives, they may gradually see an order to their lives. Those numberless events, when they occurred, may have seemed accidental at the time—people entering and leaving at certain times, traumas unfolding. But in retrospect these events become congruous elements in a consistent plot line. Just as people encountered seemingly by chance became significant agents in the structuring of a person's life story, so that person has been an agent in the structuring of other life stories. The many stories begin to fit together like one big symphony, every sound influencing and structuring every other. It's as though our lives were the story of a single storyteller, with all the characters simultaneously unfolding their stories to fit into an overall Story. For those who know God, there is a renewed realization that he was there, throughout all the chapters, patiently writing the story as it unfolded. Table 1 summarizes the developmental chapters for the "normal" family.

Chapter	Key principles	Changes needed
1. Courtship	Separating from family of origin story. Establishing own place in society.	Establish self apart from family. Develop intimate peer relationships. Establish self in work.
2. Marriage	Commitment to new family story.	Begin, with spouse, to write new story. Families of origin accept new spouse.
3. Children come	Accepting new characters into family story. Spouses able to maintain intimacy with each other.	Spouses adjust to accept new characters. Spouses assume roles as parents. Extended families assume new roles (eg., grandparents).
4. Children to school	Increasing flexibility of boundaries to include children's independence.	Children no longer dependent solely on parents. Intimacy for couple tougher to maintain ("I-ness").
5. Midlife of couple	Accepting multitude of exits/entrances into family story.	Spouses redefine characters/ roles in family story. Concern with aging parents.
6. Empty nest	Couple accepting status of being alone again.	Learn to develop adult-to-adult relationships with grown children. Renegotiate marriage now that they are no longer primarily parents. Learn how to be grandparents/ consultants. Participate in children's lives without over-involvement.
7. Retirement	Accepting the shifting of generational roles.	Maintaining own and/or couple functioning and interests in the face of declining physical abilities. Younger generation finds appropriate place for the old, using their wisdom and experience without becoming too involved. Dealing with loss of spouse, grief.

Table 1.   Developmental chapters for the "normal" family[2]

Not everyone goes through the chapters of life in this way. Spouses in second marriages may already have children (this will be discussed below). Some couples cannot or opt not to have children. A spouse may die young. If chapters in your story have decidedly deviated from the above progression, take out your journal and write the chapters (and label each).

Exercise. Take out your journal and write about the following.

1. As you watched your parents (or grandparents) face and move into retirement, how did you see them adjust to it? Was the transition to retirement relatively problem-free? Where did problems develop?

2. If you are at this time in life, reflect and write on the following: When you were young and just starting out on your own, what expectations for life did you have? Were all, some or none of these expectations met? Make a list of several of the most prominent twists your life has taken—twists that you did not expect when you were young. Reflect on each of these twists, and write how your life would have been different if they had not occurred.

A Different Twist: The Combined Family Story

Art and Sally met and fell in love, much like Bill and Mary. But there was a difference. Art and Sally both already had family stories from previous marriages. They would not have the luxury of writing the story of their marriage without constant disruptions from kids, and they needed to write a story that already included several children.

The combined family, in which couples marry and immediately assume the role of parents to each other's kids from previous marriages, offers interesting twists and turns to the couple as they write their new family story. Some people prefer to call these combined or stepfamilies until a certain amount of time has elapsed and the characters have been able to blend with one another emotionally. The couple must write their marriage relationship story while at the same time writing other critical stories:

☐ the stepparent-child story

☐ the ex-spouse story

☐ the new in-laws story

☐ the ex-in-laws story

The combined family story begins with *loss* and *grief.* A previous family story has been lost. The story line has been broken. People seem to be always coming and going. Communication is often strained. Rules seem more fluid. Although stepfamily stories look much more chaotic than those of first-time families, this by no means indicates that they are functioning less well.

Characteristics of Combined Family Stories

☐ The chapters in the combined family story don't march nicely from one to the next. In fact, the chapters may be all mixed up. For instance, if a man in his forties with two children leaving home marries a woman in her twenties with a small child, you now have a man and woman who have been writing family stories in two different chapters, dealing with two different sets of problems.

☐ Characters in this story have many expectations that the previous family story will continue unaltered in the new combined family story. Old traditions will remain the same ("We didn't do things like that before" is heard often as these families are forming).

☐ There are many conflicting loyalties. Children feel pulled between the loyalty of birth parents and stepparents. Some spouses still feel some loyalty to provide for their ex-spouses.

☐ There is no common history for all family members in the combined family. Family members have experienced different family stories in the past.

☐ There's a biological parent not on site who has power and influence. If this parent chooses to be hostile and noncompliant, chaos may soon follow.

☐ Combined family boundaries are looser than those of first-time family boundaries.

☐ The children's stories can become very confused. They are often members of two households, shuttling back and forth periodically. In one household the story unfolds one way, with certain rules, expectations and roles. Then they go off to another household and find themselves involved in a whole new story line where characters are different, the plot line is unfamiliar and expectations are completely dissimilar.

Development of the Combined Family Story

Patricia Papernow, a family researcher specializing in stepfamilies, has outlined the path that stepfamilies take on their way to writing a new family story. Each developmental stage involves tasks that must be mastered so that the family can progress onward successfully.[3] There are vast differences in how the family story is perceived, from the points of view of the remarried parent (the parent who remains with her biological children), the stepparent (the parent who enters from the outside) and each child.

Chapter 1: Getting started. In the first scene, called "Fantasy," stepfamily characters imagine instant love and togetherness that spreads healing over all the terrible wounds that have been inflicted in the past. Stepparents look at one another and imagine making their partners' lives so much easier than in the previous relationship. Both parents gaze on the children and envision becoming the perfect parents that were denied their children in previous family stories.

While the newly joined parents imagine one story, their children picture a completely different story. The cherished fantasy of many stepchildren involves reuniting their original family in a loving story (with the elimination of the evil stepparent). The new stepparent is seen as an enemy entering the child's life to snatch away something that has been cherished.

In the second scene, "Immersion," all the characters—natural parents, stepparents and children—sink into the morass of the new stepfamily. No one seems to understand the other's point of view. Tension mounts. During the third scene, "Awareness," hope is kindled in stepfamily members as the possibility of writing a whole new family story emerges.

Chapter 2: Restructuring the family story. In the first scene of this chapter, "Mobilization," conflicts emerge within the family as feelings are finally aired and discussed. From the conflict comes networks of communication. "Action" is the next scene, in which conflicts begin to be resolved. The real work of storywriting begins for the combined family, and a new story begins to emerge.

Chapter 3: The stepfamily story becomes solid. At last the combined family story comes together. During the first scene of this chapter, "Contact," the stepparent has finally become an insider in his new family. Outside influence from the off-site natural parent has diminished. And in the final scene, "Resolution," this new family can be truly called a family, not just a collection of individuals pulling in different directions. Table 2 summarizes the development of the stepfamily story.

A critical task that must be completed for the new combined family story to become well written is closure. The previous family stories from which the two spouses come must have been successfully closed. This can be extremely difficult. Divorce often leaves much bitterness (and hate is a *powerful* negative relationship that continues the old story into the future); death of a spouse and parent often goes ungrieved (leaving family members to struggle with the old story). For the divorced spouse to successfully close his or her old family story, true forgiveness must be completed—and this can be a long process. For the widowed spouse to successfully close his or her old family story, the grieving process must be completed—and this involves anger at the one who died.

Exercise. If you're currently in a combined family story, take out a large sheet of paper or newsprint. You can do this alone, or (preferably) with others in the family; you could make it a whole family project.

First draw the whole family on the paper. Draw the mother and father (you can actually draw figures, or just circles with names inside).

Now draw others who are in the constellation of this family: natural parents, grandparents, aunts, uncles. Draw lines from each person on the page to the people in your present blended family with whom each has a relationship. As you draw, discuss with whoever is present what the nature of each relationship is. (For example, "Aunt Susie only has

Chapters and scenes	Story line
Chapter 1: Getting started	The new stepfamily is in turmoil, fantasizing the best but experiencing much change and misery trying to adjust.
1. Fantasy	*Parents:* ☐ We will love each other completely. ☐ We will love our children as no one else can. ☐ Everyone in the family will be healed. *Children:* ☐ My old family will be back together again.
2. Immersion	*All family members:* I only have my own perspective, therefore ☐ I can't see your point of view. ☐ I only have my own interpretation of events. ☐ I don't even know how to talk to you. *Parents:* Overwhelmed by contradictory demands on their time, energy, loyalties. *Children:* Feelings of loss, divided loyalties.
3. Awareness	*All family members:* ☐ Begin to become aware of other family members and what each member needs/feels. ☐ Begin to get sense of where this new family story is going.
Chapter 2: Restructuring the family story	The new stepfamily story begins to take shape as family members learn new roles, conflict comes to the surface.
4. Mobilization	☐ Conflict is aired. The marriage must be strong to endure. ☐ Both spouses tire of their positions in the family (stepparent being outsider, remarried parent being in the middle).
5. Action	☐ Conflict is resolved. ☐ Family must find a way to write a new story. ☐ Bonds of prior family stories give way to emerging stepfamily story.
Chapter 3: The stepfamily story becomes solid	Family members are finally comfortable with each other, accepting each in his or her given role.
6. Contact	☐ The stepparent has moved from outsider to insider. ☐ Stepparent and stepchildren work on their relationships without interference from the remarried parent.
7. Resolution	☐ Members have the sense of being in a new family story. ☐ New rules have been put into effect. ☐ Fights of past stages are resolved.

Table 2.   The stepfamily story

a relationship with Sarah. She gives Sarah presents if Sarah will tattle on how Mommy and Steve's marriage is going.")

Next, discuss these questions.

1. Where is the combined family developmentally (young children, midlife, empty nest)?

2. Which transitions (for example, kids coming) has been the most difficult for us as a couple?

3
Your Personal Story Emerges over Time

In the last chapter we looked at Bill and Mary as they came together to start their own family story. Then their children were born. The first, a girl named Julie after Mary's grandmother Julia, was born when Mary and Bill had been married four years. Being the first, Mary and Bill doted on Julie, noting approvingly her every move and sound.

Marie followed Julie into the Simmons family four years later. Finally a son, William Jr. or Billy, was born four years after Marie. As each child began to grow, Bill and Mary were able to note his or her particular characteristics. They also watched as each child reached important stages in development.

A story develops through various chapters, over time. The chapters or stages don't vary, but the story that is written during these stages certainly varies from person to person. Actually, stories can be told from two different angles: the family story unfolding (the story of the group) and your own personal story. These stories overlap each other and are intertwined, but they are not the same story.

Your life has consisted of a number of chapters through which you have lived. In each chapter there has been a central conflict that needed to be negotiated successfully, and particular qualities that you, the hero, needed to develop with the successful resolution of the conflict.

☐ Each chapter of your personal story leads somewhat predictably to the next. Chapters cannot be skipped. Each chapter is a step toward the full ripening in adulthood of the character we become.

☐ If a child's needs aren't met at the proper time and in the proper sequence, he or she moves on without the resources necessary to take on the tasks in the chapters that will follow.

☐ As your personal story develops, you confront particular tasks and conflicts special to each chapter. If you have difficulty mastering the task and resolving the conflict, the unresolved task or conflict persists throughout your life, unfolding as a subplot in your personal story. For example, in chapter 1 hope is established, along with trust. If this is not mastered, mistrust and a sense of hopelessness follow throughout your life.

☐ Each chapter results from an interpersonal crisis, primarily with parents, but also with peers, teachers and others. A "crisis" here is not a catastrophic event but a time of heightened vulnerability and increased potential. Once a crisis is resolved in one chapter, the child moves on to the next chapter to face a new crisis.

Once each task is successfully completed, the child has established a new inner quality (ego strength) that is essential to a happy childhood and a well-rounded character. The first four of these qualities, spanning the childhood years, are hope *(I can trust my caretakers),* willpower *(I can do things on my own),* purpose *(I can initiate the action)* and competence *(I can be industrious).*

☐ Your understanding of yourself is determined primarily by your parents' actions—how they spoke to, fed, held, played with and guided you—and what they *expected* of you, laying the foundation for the formation of your character. Here your personal story and the family story intersect. Your parents are in the process of shaping a particular character (you) for the family story. Their shaping of your character, coupled with your unique responses to all the experiences you confront, go into making you the person you become (this will be discussed further in the chapter on character).

Two deviations from healthy development are common:

1. *Don't depend on anybody (grow up fast).* These people may not have had dependency needs met or weren't offered enough protection as children. These folks will never express a need. You can spot these people because they're the ones who strain to act grown-up and adequate. But they're rigid and shy away from intimacy; trust is very difficult for them. They insist that everything go their way.

2. *Always depend on everybody (don't grow up).* These folks weren't offered support to grow up and weren't given tools needed to perform the tasks at each stage. Their hidden message is *I can't do it myself (see how inadequate I am?). I must have others do it for me.*

As your personal story has unfolded, you've gone through a number of chapters (depending on your age). The discussion of each chapter below will pay particular attention to the central conflict of each chapter, what you as the hero were to have achieved as a result of the chapter, what might be a difficulty if you didn't achieve it, and how you can now compensate for what you didn't get.

Chapter 1: The Infant

Your age during this chapter: zero to nine months. This is the chapter in which your character is first introduced into the family story. Hopefully you are welcomed as an honored person in the unfolding family story.

Your primary role during this chapter: simply to *be* (to seek, accept and take in nurturing and affectionate caretaking). In this first chapter hopefully you are received and welcomed by loving parents who are there to meet your needs appropriately.

Central conflict you must face: Can you trust people and feel safe, or will you be distrustful? During the first chapter of your personal story there is one compelling need, and that is to feel safe and secure. To do this, you the infant must have a trustworthy person to whom you can be securely attached, a person who will faithfully meet your needs (holding, feeding, cleaning). If you can trust the world, you can trust yourself—your personal powers, perceptions, interpretations, feelings and desires.

If your caretakers were untrustworthy, you felt unsafe and became distrustful. You were then always on guard, needing to be in control. You may have withdrawn into yourself, becoming isolated and building walls of fear. As you grew older, intimacy was hard to develop. On the other hand, you may have become overly trusting and gullible.

Inner quality you must attain to develop your character: hope for the future. This sense of trust provides the foundation, and thus is a springboard for the child to be able in later life chapters to venture forth, secure in the knowledge that someone will be there who can be relied on.

Relationship issue you must complete: healthy narcissism and codependence. It is critical that the mothering person who first appears in your life be able to affirm that you are acceptable as an individual—you are touched, held, treated specially and adored.

The foundations of your faith are also being laid at this point, since you are learning how to trust and reach out to someone bigger than yourself. Symbols and images begin to shape conviction, and as you grow, your exposure to Bible heroes and stories is critical.

A successful first chapter	An unsuccessful first chapter
I can give/receive affection.	I can't give/receive affection
I can trust other people.	I can't trust others. I fear they'll hurt/ abandon me.
I have long-term friends.	I can't seem to keep friends.
I have good emotional and physical boundaries.	I have poor emotional and physical boundaries.
I have hope for the future.	I don't seem to have hope.

If you didn't have a successful first chapter, you'll probably find that the area you need to work on is trust. As you draw close to other people (spouse, friends, business associates), there's probably a warning signal that goes off somewhere deep inside, saying, in effect, *Danger! You're getting too close, and you're going to get hurt.* It would be very helpful for you to have a very safe person (spouse, friend) with whom you can work.

Added to feelings of trust is the need to have yourself, every part of you, affirmed as acceptable—to be loved for who you are. You are allowed to be, to exist, and that existence is celebrated.

Chapter 2: The Toddler

Your age during this chapter: nine months to three years. As your story continues, you begin to act, to look around and notice the story and the setting in which you have been placed.

Your primary role during this chapter: to *do*—to explore your world through your senses. During this chapter, tremendous curiosity wells up inside and explodes in a whirlwind of activity as you explore your world and experiment with all you find. Hopefully you are encouraged in your investigations and supported as you initiate action after action.

Central conflict you must face: developing autonomy and a sense of healthy willpower, not shame and doubt. During this time your parents need to permit you to branch out, to separate little by little from them and do more things on your own. This early exploration and discovery lays the foundation for all future creative risk-taking and adventure. Sadly, many parents are threatened with a rambunctious child who leaves their side to explore his world. Such parents often shame their children into compliance, successfully stifling the urge to taste, touch, smell, feel, hear and see what the world is about.

Inner quality you must achieve: willpower—the power of doing. You need to develop discipline at this stage, balancing between holding on and letting go. You need discipline to be free. Without healthy willpower you have no discipline: you either let go inappropriately (acting with license) or hold on inappropriately (hoarding, becoming obsessive-compulsive).

Two extremes can develop in people who have had difficulties during this chapter. Those who hurry through this chapter are constantly in a rush to do things, anything, so long as they are in constant motion. Those who never successfully complete this chapter become needy and dependent and refuse to explore their world.

Relationship issue you must complete: knowing who you are and what is yours apart from who others are and what is theirs. You need to be a separate person and express and explore your uniqueness. You hold on to your parents, at the same time saying no and generally acting oppositional. It is up to your parents to set limits and yet allow you to separate and be different.

Mother's willingness to help the child detach, first by letting him be sufficiently attached and filled with assurance of her caring presence, then by permitting him to take steps away from her, to come back and to step out again, is crucial in the development of his autonomy. If he has established trust, the toddler will now explore.

If your parents were both firm and patient, you learned that you could be angry at them and they would still be there for you. If your parents set limits, not always doing what you wanted but providing what you needed, you learned that the world was imperfect, with people having both good and bad traits.

A successful second chapter	An unsuccessful second chapter
I usually know what I want.	I have trouble knowing what I want.
I enjoy new experiences.	I'm hesitant with new experiences.
I know how to take action.	I wait for others to tell me what to do.
I appreciate my accomplishments.	I have trouble appreciating, believing in my accomplishments.
I respect people in authority.	I have frequent conflicts with people in authority.

Children are very sensitive to parents' evaluation of them. When parents are consistently reassuring, the child's sense of being accepted and valued grows. However, if parents are inconsistent in these messages or consistently devalue the child, the developing child believes that he is unworthy and unlovable. This sets the young child on a quest (sometimes lasting a lifetime) in which he desperately seeks the redemption of his lost self-esteem. This child will return again and again to the parents who have not valued him, or to someone who resembles the parents, in a desperate attempt to win approval. Unfortunately, the child often sets out on a lifetime of abusive intimate relationships.

Chapter 3: The Preschooler

Your age during this chapter: three to six years. As your story pro-
gresses, you increasingly use your mind to think, to take action, to
respond to all the world offers.

Your primary role during this chapter: to learn to *think* (become a
separate individual by testing and pushing against others). During this
act the question "why?" becomes prominent. You want to know—
everything! And everything demands an immediate explanation.

During this chapter in your life you begin to develop the power to
envision who you are and to imagine how you want to live your life.
You shower everyone with questions to learn about yourself and the
world in which you have been placed. There is so much to know and
to learn.

Central conflict you must face: developing a sense of purpose,
taking initiative, not being incapacitated by guilt. Who am I? Strength
of purpose emerges from your developing sense of identity.

If you know who you are, you can initiate and make choices. During
this chapter you stand at the center of your universe. This is not a
selfish act. You are actually incapable of seeing things from another
person's point of view. God made us this way so that we can carve out
our own identity before we begin to stand in another person's shoes.
Your father goes about the task of modeling what being a male is all
about. If you are a son, hopefully your father spends time with you so
that you can learn up close how he conducts himself as father, husband
and man. Your mother also is modeling being a female. Girls are
already bonded to their mothers and need to separate from them.

Inner quality you must achieve: purpose. You trust the world and
yourself. You are special and unique. You are a boy or a girl, and you
begin to learn how gender molds your activities. You begin to
envision your future. Purpose grows out of the unfolding awareness
of your identity.

Two extremes develop in people who have difficulties during this chapter. Those who hurry through the stage become rigid and opinionated, pushing fear into the shadows and refusing to depend on anyone. Those who stall during this act give up control of themselves, avoid taking positions or opinions and generally assume a charming, agreeable posture.

Relational issue you must complete: independence. As you mold your own separateness as a person, you begin to break bonds of dependency and establish boundaries between yourself and others. You find the limits of acceptable behavior. You begin to form your own opinion on certain matters. You develop control. You learn to push against others and deal with the reactions this causes.

Your parents, as their lives unfold together, model an intimate relationship (for better or for worse) between mates. Perhaps you came from a family where mother and father modeled healthy closeness and partnership. Or you may have come from a family story in which parents did not display love toward each other. This may have left you with a hesitancy about being close to another person.

I have written a book, *Questions Couples Ask Behind Closed Doors* (Tyndale, 1996), in which I discuss specifically how intimacy can be learned by those who have experienced poor modeling.

A successful third chapter	An unsuccessful third chapter
I can plan and initiate projects and take responsibility for them.	I can't plan and initiate action. It's hard for me to take responsibility for my actions.
I feel good about myself as a boy/girl. I have healthy attitudes about sex.	I have difficulties considering myself as a boy/girl. I am conflicted about sex.
I appreciate my parents and their relationship (though I don't agree with all they did).	I am disturbed by many things in my parents' relationship and do not want to emulate them in any way.
I am comfortable with my feelings and those of people around me.	I am uncomfortable with my feelings and try to control the feelings of others around me.
I can laugh and have fun.	I have difficulty laughing. Life seems very much a drudgery.

Chapter 4: The School-Ager

Your age during this chapter: six years to puberty. It is a big step to leave home for the first time and head off to school. This new phase in your life means that you are now entering a new world where the learning and socializing begun at home will continue. Hopefully you have successfully incorporated the earlier ego strengths: trust and hope, autonomy and willpower, initiative and purpose. Now it is time for you to learn the socialization skills—cooperation, interdependence and healthy competition—you will need throughout life.

Your primary role during this chapter: to *discover* your identity—to establish who you are within a network of social relationships. You are discovering who you are and what it means to be a male or a female. At the same time you learn to separate fantasy from reality.

Central conflict you must face: developing competence from industry, not sinking into a sense of inferiority. During this chapter you experiment with different ways of doing things, making many mistakes in the process. All the while you are developing various physical, intellectual, emotional and social skills. Many of the morals and values that will guide you the rest of your life are being framed.

Inner quality you must achieve: competence. Productivity involves planning and execution. Other desires and interests must be held in check while a planned task is successfully completed. During this time the older generations teach the younger generations the skills necessary to get on successfully in the world, then challenge them to reach toward accomplishments.

Self-esteem is built on two things: challenging work within a disciplined, loving environment. Competence is the first cousin of self-esteem, for when I feel competent (having met and successfully overcome challenges) I will indeed have healthy self-esteem.

Children tend to be more competent at earlier ages than adults give them credit for. Hopefully your parents encouraged you to stretch beyond what they may have thought you were capable of doing. If your parents helped you set goals, then linked *sustained effort*—not ability—with success, you probably have been able to equate effort, not ability, with success.

Those who hurry through this life chapter tend to avoid the testing necessary to establish who they are, thus becoming fixed and rigid in a belief that may not be accurate. Those who become dependent may become afraid of thinking and doing for themselves and may seek out others to do their thinking for them.

Relational issue you must complete: interdependence and cooperation. Your mind begins to be able to think logically, but still concretely (not until adolescence will you be able to think abstractly about propositions). With your mind you perform academic tasks, gaining a sense of power as new abilities are developed.

During this time in your life, play is one of the most serious "jobs" you have. Many people don't realize the critical role that play has in the developing life of the youngster.

A successful fourth chapter	An unsuccessful fourth chapter
I appreciate my strengths and weaknesses.	I have trouble assessing weaknesses and strengths. I doubt when others point these out to me.
I experience healthy give-and-take in conflict.	I give in completely *or* always must have my way in conflicts.
I can follow projects through to completion.	I have difficulty completing projects.
I know when to take responsibility for my actions.	I tend to shift blame to others when things go wrong.
I have a number of achievements I can point to with pride.	It's hard for me to think of anything I've done competently.

Chapter 5: The Adolescent

Your age during this chapter: thirteen to twenty-one. With puberty, childhood comes to an end. This chapter offers you far-reaching opportunities to solidify all the previous chapters into a strong sense of self.

Your primary role during this act: to *unify* your personality (to develop as a mature psychosexual person). This chapter is a bridge in your unfolding personal story, a bridge between the chapters of childhood and the chapters of adulthood (see 1 Cor 13:11). Seeds are sown during this chapter that will sprout into a new beginning in young adulthood.

The successful adolescent is one who is able to gather up her genetic abilities, integrate these with the ego strengths and skills she has been developing throughout earlier life chapters, and avail herself of the opportunities that society offers her.

Central conflict you must face: developing your sense of identity, not falling into role confusion. The quest to discover identity—*who am I?*—actually continues into, and in many cases throughout, the years of the twenties. This sense of identity will spring from two main sources: significant love relationships (friendships and marriage) and vocation (the work to which one is called and equipped).

This life chapter is marked by a great deal of ambivalence. On the one hand you are desperately reaching for independence and separation from parents; on the other you are nervously retreating back into the more familiar confines of childhood behaviors.

Inner quality you must achieve: fidelity. This is a chapter in your personal story that receives much attention. That's because during this chapter you will hopefully solidify who you are as a person and prepare to launch off to write your own family story. If the turmoil can be successfully negotiated, there is an inner and outer sense of fidelity, faithfulness to who you are as a person and loyalty to those around you who now form your significant community.

Relational issue you must complete: independence from family. During this chapter it is very important that you perform the difficult task of separating (not just physically but also emotionally) from your family-of-origin story. It's not that you will ever be completely "written out" of this story. You'll always play a role in it. But now it is time to establish your own story apart from that family story. Included in your new story, we hope, is the finding of and developing of a place in the grown-up world.

In relation to faith, the young person ideally is piecing together a personal philosophy that includes four elements:

1. I am the creation of God. I have certain unique abilities, talents and capacities that make me distinct from everyone else.

2. I am a child of God. Because of this, I have been given certain gifts. There is one primary gift I have been given, and several secondary gifts that supplement and enhance the primary gift. These gifts form the basis for the contributions I will ultimately make in life.

3. I am a servant of God. I have a special calling.

4. I am gifted by God. I know in what areas I will be able to make contributions to the Christian community and within my vocational calling.

A successful fifth chapter	An unsuccessful fifth chapter
I have a good sense of who I am.	I am confused about who I am.
I do age-appropriate activities with people my own age.	People frequently tell me to "grow up." I prefer people younger than myself.
I know my core beliefs and have thought them through.	I'm unsure of what I believe, and tend to go along with the crowd.
I can respect other people's point of view.	I need to be right all the time and have difficulty seeing issues from others' viewpoint.
I can express an opinion, even when it goes against popular opinion.	I usually go along with the crowd and have difficulty disagreeing with popular opinions.

Chapter 6: The Young Adult

Your age during this chapter: twenty-two to forty. As you venture forth into the adult world, two major goals loom ahead: love and vocation.

Your primary role during this chapter: to *reach out*—to connect with others in lasting relationships. The quest for identity (chapter 5) usually continues simultaneously with this chapter, which is the quest for close relationships. During this chapter you must attend to two stories. In your personal story, you need to focus your energies on a story theme—what your story will be about. At the same you need to begin reaching out to form a relationship with another person, with a view toward writing a whole new family story.

Your focus narrows as you discover who you are. Your understanding of your gifts is what narrows the focus. Now you must begin to develop a story theme. Stephen Covey speaks of the theme (what he calls a "mission statement") as a combination of character (what you want to be) and contributions (what you want to do).[1] Life is prioritized as you center on who you are, then on what you want to do.

Michael is a young man in his late twenties who came to me not long ago. He was immensely talented and had already made a great deal of money while establishing a solid reputation in his career field. He had worked several years for two different firms. He was married and had two children. Yet Michael lacked focus. As he sat before me, he framed his question: "I just don't know what I'm all about, what I'm supposed to be doing with my life. I spend a lot of time at work. I enjoy my children immensely. But I can't really say I know what I'm really supposed to be doing with my life."

Michael is struggling with several of the issues of this life chapter. He has formed an intimate relationship, married and begun a family. But he questions his vocation, what he is best gifted to do in his life. He has apprenticed in two different jobs, but as yet he does not have an abiding sense of vocation. During this chapter, a mentor or mentors will be extremely helpful both vocationally and spiritually to help him settle these questions and continue writing a successful story.

Central conflict you must face: developing intimacy, not isolation. You are beginning to reach out toward others more deeply and seriously. Though not all people will find themselves married and beginning new family stories, hopefully you will be reaching out to form deep, lasting bonds of friendship that will satisfy your needs for togetherness and closeness.

Inner quality you must achieve: love. Love has several faces, and during this chapter it is important that you discover these faces as you connect with other people in close associations. There is the love of close, abiding friendship, a love that seeks the good of another as it draws you close to that person *(philia)*. There is the love of community that draws you into close associations with others for the common good of the group *(storgē)*. There is the love that wills to reach out to another to complete the self and bond with that person *(eros)*. And finally, there is the love that goes beyond the needs of the self and ultimately reflects God's love for us, in that this love is completely unselfish and self-giving *(agapē)*.

Relational issue you must complete: forming a lasting, committed relationship. After God had made everything and declared it good, he said, "It is not good for the man to be alone" (Gen 2:18). This is not necessarily a statement about marriage per se, but it stresses the need to be closely related to another person, to share, to interact. The book of Ruth gives us pictures of two key intimate relationships that hold up society: friendship (Naomi and Ruth) and marriage (Ruth and Boaz).

As you progress through your twenties and into your thirties, the question arises, Do I want to continue my commitments to my relationships? The demands of occupation may cause you to put your relational obligations on the back burner, so that these relationships suffer.

Faith, during this stage, has hopefully matured to the point where you are able to enter fully into community with others, giving and receiving as gifts are exercised. This is also a time to be mentored spiritually. It will be ideal if you can find a mature Christian person who can come alongside and point the way spiritually.

A successful sixth chapter	An unsuccessful sixth chapter
I have a number of close friends with whom I can share on a deep level.	I'm basically a loner. I rarely let acquaintances get to know me.
I am comfortable when my friends are involved in activities with other people.	I want my friends to do things only with me.
I have been able to establish a committed love relationship.	I am afraid of love relationships and shy away from them.
I have become an active member of a church and/or community organization.	I have not joined any organizations; I shy away from these affiliations.
I can articulate my faith and my personal philosophy of life.	I cannot articulate my faith, and I have little sense of a personal philosophy.

Chapter 7: The Midlifer

Age during this chapter: forty-one to sixty-five. Some would say that this chapter in your story is actually a return to many of the struggles you faced as an adolescent: Who am I? What is life all about? And what is my place in this unfolding story?

Your primary role during this chapter: to *persevere*—to keep adjusting the focus on your calling. As you move through the thirties and into midlife, a number of dangers lurk. One of the most prominent

is *dabbling*—where the person undertakes a number of ventures with
only a shallow degree of commitment to each pursuit followed. The
work of identity for this person was never completed, and the person
has a faulty view of his vocation. As a result, the person does not have
a focus in life. Therefore his task now is to gain focus by discovering
and utilizing the gifts God has given him.

The second danger at this age is *plateauing*—that is, deciding to
stop learning and hence to stop growing. But once you stop growing,
you have sown the seeds of death.

Central conflict you must face: developing a sense of generativity,
not stagnation. During this chapter you will come to terms with the
past *(what have I done to this point?)* and set your course for the future
(what do I do now?). As you go through the process of recalibrating
your life's course, you need to make certain choices, set certain
priorities. This process begins with your premise *(what's my story
about?),* which involves who you want to be *(what's my character?)*
and then what you want to do *(what are my contributions and achievements?).*

Inner quality you must achieve: care—to take responsibility for
another person, to feel concern for another. Achieving this can be
tough, especially when you have apparently reentered adolescence in
search of your identity. But the need to stay connected and to focus on
the needs of others is critical at times when the struggling midlifer
would rather crawl into a cave and contemplate his or her own life for
a year or two.

Relational issue you must complete: maintaining the commitment
in relationship through the stresses and strains of life. As your children
grow, become less dependent and eventually move out on their own,
you find yourself without the mediating presence of children to defuse
pressures and conflicts with your spouse. During this chapter some
couples find that they have nothing to say to each other, and the
marriage flounders.

You may also find that your parents are growing into old age,
becoming increasingly dependent on you for support. Decisions need

to be made about their care and comfort.

In your developing faith, this is a time for mentoring. As you move through the middle years successfully, you reach a time when you are ready to begin to invest in the lives of younger people who are now following you, developing their own unique stories.

A successful seventh chapter	An unsuccessful seventh chapter
I think of new ideas and projects that I want to carry out.	I feel as though my mind is on hold, and I can't generate new ideas.
I mentor other people entering my field of expertise.	I tend to ignore young people who are entering my profession.
I enjoy innovations and new experiences at church and out in the community.	I fight against anything new and wish nothing would change.
I can make new choices and commitments about the direction of the rest of my life.	I seem unable to make choices and feel stuck in ruts.
I enjoy a number of areas where I am learning new things.	I have stopped learning new things.

Chapter 8: The Senior

Your age during this chapter: sixty-five to death. This is the final chapter in your story, when you look back over all you have done and tie up the loose ends, but also accept new challenges.

Your primary role during this chapter: to *complete*—to look back on your life story with satisfaction, while still writing the final pages.

In your later years, as you reflect back over your individual story and the family stories of which you've been a part, you will see how the pieces of the story fit together. When you are in the midst of a painful, complicated situation, it is usually impossible to understand why it is happening, how this event fits into the whole. But in retrospect, the pieces will usually fit.

People usually think of David's great poem, Psalm 23, as having been written when he was a shepherd boy watching his father's sheep. Judging from the experiences David relates in the poem—walking through the valley of the shadow of death, sitting down with enemies—I think that it was written by a much older David. I suggest he is in the twilight of his life, looking back over the story of his life. As an older man, he can see the Great Shepherd leading him beside still waters and restoring his soul after extreme hardships. He can remember how he was in the valley of the shadow of death, with the Lord at his side. And now that he is old, David turns around and sees the personifications of goodness and mercy following along behind him. They've been following through all the pages of his story. And now his story trails off into the house of the Lord, where his story will continue to unfold forever.

Central conflict you must face: developing a sense of integrity, not despair. It's not that all the loose ends of your story are neatly tied up when you reach your dotage. Many of the tragedies you have faced—the baby who died in infancy, the brother lost in the war, the financial reversal that seemed to come at the worst possible time—may never have a satisfactory explanation in your unfolding story. That's why C. S. Lewis stated that the word spoken most often in heaven will be *oh*—as in "Oh, now I see." We realize here on earth, as our stories unfold, that we see through a glass darkly. But as Paul says in his first letter to the Corinthians, when we stand face to face with the Savior, the pieces of the story will finally come together.

In this perspective on life's story, the true benefit of having elders among us becomes plain. People who have lived through most of their story, who have weathered the complications, who have fit the pieces together, can explain to younger folks the rhythm and pacing that become evident in each person's story.

Western Christians are so impatient, so prone to jump to conclusions, so anxious to get to the bottom line in each unfolding story. The older generation can add the vital component of patience and perseverance to the understandings of younger generations. Not all the loose ends in our stories can be neatly tied up and interpreted. But the seniors among us can show how God has been at work, even in the darkest hours.

Inner quality you must achieve: wisdom. Wisdom is ultimately a perspective, a way of seeing and understanding our unfolding stories. During this last chapter of life, you reread the story you have been writing through the years, and hopefully you are now able to see each chapter through God's eyes. You are also able now to interpret your story in light of the unfolding Story that God is writing, to understand how the pieces all fit into the larger narrative.

Relational issue you must complete: saying goodbye to your most significant relationships. When Mickey Mantle, former baseball star with the New York Yankees, was dying, he took time to look back over his life and his relationships. "I wasn't a good family man," he said, recalling the years he ignored his wife and four sons while drinking heavily and doing as he pleased as a sports hero. But as Mantle's health failed and he finally gave up alcohol, he was able to focus on the truly important things. "For all those years I lived the life of somebody I didn't know. A cartoon character. From now on, Mickey Mantle is going to be a real person. I still can't remember much of the last 10 years . . . but I'm looking forward to the memories I'll have in the next 10."[2]

St. Paul had a very different assessment of his life as the end drew near. "I have fought the good fight, I have finished the race, I have kept the faith. Now there is in store for me the crown of righteousness, which the Lord, the righteous Judge, will award to me on that day" (2 Tim 4:7-8).

Spiritually, it is a time for finishing well. Following is a summary of how Paul Stanley, vice president of the Navigators, describes those who finish well:

1. They had perspective that enabled them to bring into focus the story that has already unfolded. As events now happen, or as there is reflection over past occurrences, they can see the broader context and hence can relate these to a greater purpose.

2. They enjoyed intimacy with Christ and experienced repeated times of inner renewal. They have drawn ever closer to Christ through the complications of life, experiencing his love and comfort, seeking his forgiveness and refreshment.

3. They were disciplined in important areas of life. "Bringing any God-given talent, gift or opportunity to full maturity and fruitfulness demands discipline." Those who finish well have applied discipline to avoid mediocrity and failure.

4. They maintained a positive learning attitude all their life. Some allow themselves to become lax after formal education and training cease; but the person who finishes well is always researching new areas, discovering new truths, applying new learnings.

5. They had a network of meaningful relationships and several important mentors during their lifetime. Those who finish well are well connected. They have developed and maintained relationships, whether with family members, friends, mentors or colleagues, as a priority throughout their lives.

A successful eighth chapter	An unsuccessful eighth chapter
I can reflect back over my life with a great deal of satisfaction about things accomplished.	I have many regrets about my life and find myself ruminating over what I should have done.
I enjoy a good reputation in my community.	My reputation in the community is not as good as I would like.
I find new channels for my talents and abilities.	I cannot seem to channel my energy productively.
I manage my time and financial resources effectively.	I have trouble managing my time and finances.
I find that I can change my actions and attitudes with changing circumstances.	I find that I am rigid in my actions and attitudes, and cannot seem to change.

Life chapter	Role	Conflict	Inner quality	Relationship
The infant	To be	Trust vs. mistrust	Hope	Narcissism Codependence
The toddler	To do	Autonomy vs. shame/doubt	Willpower	Counterdependence
The preschooler	To think	Initiative vs. guilt	Purpose	Independence
The schoolager	To discover	Industry vs. inferiority	Competence	Interdependence
The adolescent	To unify	Identity vs. role confusion	Fidelity	Independence from family
The young adult	To reach out	Intimacy vs. isolation	Love	Committed relationship
The midlifer	To persevere	Generativity vs. stagnation	Care	Maintain commitment
The senior	To complete	Integrity vs. despair	Wisdom	Say goodby

Table 3. A review of your story's chapters

Women's Development

Development theorists have begun to rethink many of the categories I have listed above as being the norm for both men and women. Carol Gilligan, the most prominent theorist in female development, centers women's development on a struggle for connection.[3] Women tend to define themselves in relationships and in connections to other people. Because of this, women can be seen to have difficulty with separation and individuation.

Men and women therefore develop from opposite directions and feel vulnerable at the opposite ends:

☐ Men feel vulnerable connecting and have trouble with intimacy.

☐ Women feel vulnerable separating and have trouble with autonomy.

Because developmental literature is heavily weighted toward the separation issue, women's failure to separate is seen as a failure to develop. Until psychology is able to create better chapters for the woman's developmental experience, we will be left with an incomplete picture.

Men	Women
Separation and autonomy: "I stand alone"	Affiliation and relationship: "I stand in relationship"
Identity, then intimacy	Identity tied to intimacy
Competition	Cooperation
Minimize emotions	Helper and caretaker
Hard to identify feelings	Self-aware of feelings
Development = coming to see the other as equal to self; discovery that equality provides a way of making connections safe	Development = inclusion of self in expanding network of connection; discovery that separation can be protective, needn't involve isolation
Moral development = hierarchy; begins with separateness, explores connection	Moral development = network; begins with connection, explores separateness

Exercises. 1. Draw a line, similar to the one below, to show the significant events of your life—those leading up to your birth, then from your birth onward to today. You might want to organize the events according to the chapters described above. Now extend the line from today until the time of your death. Under this section of the line write down your goals and aspirations, the dreams and ambitions that you hope to accomplish before your death.

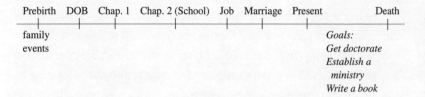

2. Go down through the list of qualities that emerge at each stage of development. Put a check beside those that seem to be a problem for you right now. Note in your journal those qualities that you have been able to greatly improve over the years.

Quality to be achieved	
I can trust other people.	
I know what I want in most areas of my life (physically, emotionally, mentally, spiritually).	
I can initiate actions and take responsibility for these actions.	
I can appreciate my accomplishments.	
I know who I am and feel comfortable with this knowledge.	
I can be close to other people.	
I can continue to generate new ideas and activities.	
I can look over my life with satisfaction.	

3. Look at the chart on page 85. In the first column, list the significant times in your personal life story (you may or may not use the chapters I have described). Then think of and list the specific events that happened during each significant period. Next write in the people who were important to you during those events, then the emotional impact that each event had on you. Last, write in the decisions you made as a consequence of these events.

Significant period	Events	People	Emotional impact	Decisions made

4

The Story's Characters

So these are the *Simmons children,* I thought to myself.
Bill and Mary Simmons had spoken of them during the two counseling
sessions I'd had with them. It was the crisis with young Bill that had
brought the couple to counseling in the first place. Now I got a chance
to see for myself what these people were all about. I thought it would
be helpful to hear from everyone in this family, to see how each
understood the family story.

There were three children. Oldest daughter Julie, nearing thirty, had
done everything "perfectly" throughout life. She was now married to
the perfect man and had two wonderful children. Today she sat next
to her father.

Second daughter Marie was not quite as perfect. She was somewhat
passive and, at twenty-six, was just now beginning to get her life in
order and get out into the world. As a teenager she'd had a baby out
of wedlock and given it up for adoption. Today she sat near her mother.

The youngest, only son Billy Jr., age twenty and the focus of all the
attention, was obviously the family rebel. Today he sat across from
everyone, glaring at them all.

"So you're the psychologist who's been seeing my parents." Julie
spoke up even before I had a chance to introduce myself.

"Yes, I am. I wanted to have you all come in and see what each of you feel about this family and what has gone wrong in the past several months."

"Several months?" Billy broke in. "Try ten years!"

Everyone in the family moved immediately to settle young Bill down and soften his words. This was obviously a family that was not used to airing its dirty linen, at least not in public.

"I won't be silent," Billy went on belligerently. "This family hides everything behind Dad's pulpit. Well, it's time we admit to the world that we're flawed, that we have problems. Hey, look at me"—Billy rose to his feet for effect—"I'm practically a convicted felon. Get a load of that."

"Billy, sit down. You're upsetting Mother and embarrassing Father." Julie stepped in to take charge, as was evidently her customary role with her siblings.

It was apparent from the beginning that Julie basked in the admiration of both her parents, but especially her father. She was the oldest, the first child, the first daughter. She had excelled in everything—academics (on every honor roll and dean's list until she graduated magna cum laude), cheerleading, community activism. Now she was the perfect wife and mother to two darling children. In fact, Julie seemed to embody everything that both Mary and Bill had always hoped to be themselves but were never quite able to accomplish. In some ways Julie had been glued to a pedestal in her family; I suspected that she was confined there, unable to blossom in directions that would have been more satisfying to her.

And here was young Bill, the rebel, his potential lost, parental hopes dashed. He had made a career of doing the exact wrong thing at the right time. He had been named for his father, of course. But oddly enough, this boy seemed to have a knack for doing everything exactly opposite of what his father had done down through his unfolding life's story.

And finally Marie, who was lost in the family shuffle, her quiet voice drowned out by louder family members. Her accomplishments were hidden behind the accolades heaped on her sister and the gunfire elicited by her brother. This middle child had evidently caught much of the internal drama from her mother, who seemingly had never really resolved her own poor adolescent decisions. Marie had made a number of significant decisions similar to her mother's. Her name, Marie, had come from her grandmother, who, like Mary and now Marie, had become pregnant out of wedlock after immigrating to the United States from Greece.

We talked further of Julie's perfections, of Billy's rebellions. Finally I came to Marie and asked her to tell me her story, so that I would not be added to the list of those who ignored her.

"In the family I'm called Foggy," she told me. "I'm not sure how I came to be called this name, but I can tell you I can't stand it." Marie cast her glance down to the floor. "It started with my brother, I think," she continued. "He began to call me London Fog, or just Fog or Foggy. For some reason he got it in his head that I was a ditz. Then I had an uncle who started calling me London. It was awful. That was before I was a teenager. And here I am at my age, and they still call me this.

"I think I'm a pretty competent person, at least in most things I try. But around my family"—at the mention of her family she drew her limbs in closer to her body—"I *am* a ditz. I get tentative. When they ask me a question, my mouth goes dry, and I can't really force out a good answer. I can't seem to make a rational decision."

Have you ever wondered why you were named for your father, Simon Eastman Forrest III? or for your Aunt Minnie? or for that famous Civil War general? or that actress? Did you think it was because your parents liked the sound of the name? Perhaps. But more than likely there were other forces at work, forces that continue at work in the shaping of your character, and ultimately in the writing of your story.

The Original Character

You were created by God with particular characteristics, because God wanted to include you as a character ultimately in his Story. I'll call this your *original self*. Your original self is made up of all your parts, all facets of your personality, in place originally as God created you to be. God wove into your being all the particular characteristics that would perfectly blend to make you his special person.

So why aren't we the special people God created us to be? Why do we display so little of the original self? Obviously something has gone very wrong. How has this process then worked in each of us to deface us, to mar the original self God created?

The Refashioned Character
The original self God created us to be was refashioned along the way—ultimately because we live in a fallen world. How did this happen?

Parents, as the primary refashioners of our character, reach into their minds' storehouses, take out parts of their internal drama (hopes, dreams, conflicts, character traits denied to them) and place these onto their children. These are parts that have not been successfully dealt with and integrated into the parent, or parts that haven't previously developed, or parts that the parent likes about herself and wishes to see developed in her child. When we have great difficulty understanding one of our children, he usually exhibits parts of us that are less known to us, parts we find scary and undeveloped. Someone once said that the greatest burden the child must bear is the unlived life of his parents.

This process unfortunately reworks the original self of the child into another character (the refashioned self), one suited to the story the parents are writing. One day the actor Burt Reynolds was interviewed by Katie Couric on the *Today Show*. Speaking of his three-year-old son, he said, "There's a lot of things I did when I was young that I hope my son won't repeat. But I have this feeling that he's going to."[1] This boy has barely had time to walk the earth, and already his father is "seeing" traits emerging. Unfortunately, the net result is that we create our children more in our own image than in God's intended image. Let's look at this process to see exactly how the characters in the family story are fashioned.

1. We look at our children and note certain behaviors. Children exhibit myriad behaviors, sounds, expressions, gestures; but certain ones of these jump out at us.

I remember when my daughter was born. I was one of the first fathers that our local hospital allowed in the delivery room. Mandy began screaming, as most children do when they are born. I fixated on that scream, and I liked it. *Well, she certainly has a good pair of lungs on her,* I thought. What I perceived as her extroversion, her ability to articulate her feelings, wasn't really there. The only thing present at that point was a baby who was screaming. The rest of my assessment came from my own head, my storehouse of characters and traits, what I hope for and dream of.

2. Once we identify certain behaviors in each of our children, we make the leap of describing these behaviors as manifestations of particular characteristics. Throughout their growing-up years, then, we constantly remind ourselves and our children that they are in fact exhibiting the characteristics we've ascribed to them. "You are such a clown." "You're Mama's little helper." "I can't believe you're so poor with your hands."

"Look at Johnny jerk his arm out like that," a proud father said as he gazed at his infant son. "I just know he's going to quarterback the Forty-niners." Well, Junior may quarterback the Forty-niners, but at six months of age, the jerking arm has more to do with reflexes than with intentional passing movements.

3. As we identify with our children, we parent from the position of what we sense our child to be. "She's like me. She feels the way I feel." We've reached into the storehouse in our mind, pulled out characters and characteristics that have been important to us in the past, and placed them on our child.

4. So here we are as parents, seeing ourselves (or possibly others we've known) in our kids. As our children grow, we begin to remind them of the particular characters we expect them to develop into. "I know you're going to be just like me." Our kids respond by demonstrating the behavior that confirms to us how much they really *are* like

us, and we start trying to help them with all those bad feelings we
sense they're feeling. (They may be, but more often than not it's really
feelings we had long ago or now that we think we've identified in our
kid.)
    5. There are several consequences.

☐ My child has God-given characteristics that would be important to
develop, but they're not celebrated and needed in the family story, so they
get lost in the shadows, tucked away in the child's storehouse. Examples
of children who might experience this: the gregarious child in the
introverted family; the athletic child in the intellectual family; the extremely intuitive child in the sensory-based family.

☐ I misinterpret much of my child's behavior and feelings, assigning
characteristics and moods that really aren't there, but *need* to be there
to give meaning to the child's behavior and continuity to the family story.

☐ I create my child more in my image than in the image God intended.
My story takes precedence over God's Story.

☐ I can't set limits appropriately. I reason, *He's (I've) been hurt
enough!* As you identify increasingly with your child, you begin to
transmit information to him—*This is the character that I need in the
story I'm writing. So here's your script. Go to it.*

☐ I may even drag the child in to deflect the conflict that simmers
between my spouse and me. Warring couples are very unstable and
tend to try to draw others in to change the terms of the struggle.
Children standing around are perfect for this duty. A child who is being
fashioned for a particular role in the family may find himself pulled
again and again into a conflict that actually is between his parents.

    The relationship between Mary Simmons and her daughter Marie
reflects some of these tendencies. Mary never resolved her own
out-of-wedlock pregnancy and the inadequacy in her life that had
foreshadowed that event. As a result, the elements of her story,
including key components of her personality, were resurrected, projected onto Marie, and replayed in Marie's emerging personal story
(which now is also an critical part of the Simmons family story).

    Recently a troubled family came in for counseling. The teenage boy had been using drugs and had become sexually involved with his girlfriend. The father looked at him and launched into a litany that went something like this: "I've seen it for a long time. You're just like my brother Steve. He's never been able to follow through on anything. He just bums around the country mooching off of other people. He can't hold a job, can't stay in a relationship . . ."

At this point I cut the father off, because it appeared that the father was describing *and* predicting what his son was to become. This whole characterization indeed was the process I needed to interrupt so that the boy could develop a new story with a wholly different character.

The original parts of ourselves, those that God made but that were ignored and suppressed by parents and others, don't just cease to be. They're still there, but tucked away from consciousness in what I've called the storehouse in one's mind. As we grow, if these parts remain undeveloped or at least unexamined, they become prime candidates to be projected onto our children once we grow up and marry.

Naming and Molding

Parents, as they mold in their child a self that is something other than the original self God created, assume they're fashioning the original self. But the self they are actually fashioning is made up mainly of characteristics that emerge from themselves, not innately from the child. These are traits the parents value, approve of and understand (which creates a much approved-of child). Or they may be traits that were lost to the parents long ago—submerged in the parents' lost selves and buried in the storehouse of their minds. The children bearing these traits tend to be the "black sheep," the misunderstood children, the children who develop problems.

In the ancient Hebrew culture, parents' naming of their children was a formal process. Names were not simple designations. They were *descriptions*. Parents looked at the child and named according to what they saw. The classic example of this is Jacob, who was born holding on to the ankle of his twin brother Esau. There's a good chance that mother Rebekah, seeing the infant grasping his brother's heel, was reminded of her own brother, Laban. Laban was a cheat and a scoundrel, but Rebekah loved him anyway. I venture to guess that Rebekah was the instigator of the name Jacob *(He's a supplanter like my brother!).*

But a name was not just a description; it was also a prediction: *I see you doing this. I also expect that you will do this in the future.* When Jacob grabbed hold of his brother's ankle, his parents assumed that he was trying to gain the upper hand over his brother. Both parents assumed that young Jacob would continue to manifest this type of behavior. Of course Jacob lived up to his parents' expectations and did just that.

A NAME = A DESCRIPTION + A PREDICTION

Several factors play in as parents begin to assign characteristics ("name") and then dispense roles to their children.

Birth Order

Over and over I've heard the same lament: "We were both raised in the same family—how could we be so different?" The truth is, no one was raised in the same family! Each member experiences the emerging family story differently, depending on their particular place in it. One of the most important factors that influence characteristics among siblings is the order in which they were born. Now, it's possible to become too mechanical in discussing sibling position, so that it becomes like an astrological predictor. But understanding this element of family life is very helpful for understanding how people deal with important relationships when they become adults.

Jerome Bach and his colleagues researched birth order in relation to the needs of an unfolding family story.[2] Bach contends that every family story has four basic needs:

- ☐ the need for productivity
- ☐ the need for emotional maintenance
- ☐ the need for relationship
- ☐ the need for unity

These needs are handled by each child born to the family according to his or her birth order, Bach says. Walter Toman, another researcher in birth order, has added further insights.[3] Putting together the insights of Bach and Toman, let's consider several of the factors in birth order.

Firstborn and only children. If you were the first or only child to be born to your parents, you are in fact your parents' experiment in parenting. Everything was new for your parents—a crying baby, changing diapers, walks around the block, childhood illnesses.

Firstborns receive their parents' undivided attention, for better and for worse. Every gurgle and smile is noted and cherished. Great care is taken to ensure that all is well for the firstborn. Humorist Erma Bombeck put it this way: "When my first child was born, when she dropped her bottle on the floor, I would quickly pick it up and sterilize it before returning it to the baby. By the time my fifth child came along, that child had to wrestle the dog for the bottle."

Because there are no other siblings around, firstborns identify primarily with parents and thus conform much more readily to parental demands and values. They become used to exerting great effort in living up to adult expectations, so when they go off to school they often bring home better report cards than their younger brothers and sisters. In most ways firstborns pave the way for their younger siblings, setting the standards by which all those who follow will be measured.

Only children never have to compete with siblings for attention. They remain at the center always, getting whatever support is needed at a moment's notice. The day-to-day give-and-take of sharing life with someone of one's generation is a foreign idea to them. Hence only children often relate much better to superiors than to peers. They also do best when they are the center of attention. Bach points out that only children often carry all the family story's basic needs; this makes for strong functioning when the family story is well written, but it is disastrous when the story is poorly written.

Bach observes that firstborn kids bear the productivity needs of the family, so they carry more performance expectations. This child identifies most with the father, who can be seen as the production manager. He or she will hold values identical to or exactly opposite of the father's. This child also carries the family's dominant values and story themes.

Firstborns tend to be socially aware and conform readily to social norms. These folks also tend to see issues as black-and-white and abide by the letter of the law over the spirit of it.

Middle children. Children in the middle tend to be gregarious and more dependent on the approval of peers than that of adults. Feeling like outsiders in their own families, they turn to friends outside the family. They are extremely loyal and will tolerate unfulfilling situations longer than their siblings.

Middle children have watched as their older counterparts negotiated through the family thickets, so middles learn from observing those experiences. Middles are more indulged and held less responsible than firstborns, who often are placed in charge of younger siblings and thus forced to assume responsibilities.

Middles tend to have an easier time separating from parents and forging their own identities, because their parents' attention has already been somewhat modulated by the older sibling.

Bach observed that middles are especially attuned to the emotional needs of the family story. They resonate with the covert rules that pulsate through the family story. They pick up the family's emotional undertones quickly, but have trouble understanding what they themselves are feeling. Their principal focus is on the mother, with whom they identify or to whom they react, thus making their decisions in sympathy with or in reaction to the mother's deepest values. Often these children become extensions of the mother's unconscious needs and desires.

Third children. Bach concluded that these children are most attuned to the relationship needs of the family story. In particular, they hook into the parents' marriage relationship and thus become a symbol of what is occurring there.

Fourth children assume the unity needs of the family story. This child picks up tension as it grows within the family, takes responsibility for it, then attempts to defuse it with distractions. This child often becomes the family entertainer or mascot in order to deflect the pain.

Bach thought that the *fifth child* in the family acted like the first child again, the sixth like the second, and so forth. Toman went to great lengths to discuss the effects of sex of the child combined with birth order, such as an oldest male with female sisters.

Sex of the child. Not only is birth order important as parents shape character, but the sex of the child is also critical in this process. The first girl born in a family, no matter what the birth order, takes on a significance different from that of the first boy born in a family.

To complicate the matter more, parents' experience with their own siblings when they were growing up exerts a powerful influence on each child. For instance, Dave was the oldest son and had two younger brothers. He never had the opportunity of interacting with sisters, so he had no experience with young girls' behavior as they are developing. Now Dave has his own family. First a girl is born, and he is delighted with her. In many ways she is a novelty to him. But then a son is born to Dave and his wife. Now Dave is able to unleash all his special love and attention.

A third child born to the family is another girl, who is all but ignored by father Dave. The oldest daughter becomes Mom's special helper and friend—junior mother in some ways. The middle boy becomes Dave's special friend as the two go off to play sports and do "guy things." The youngest daughter becomes the lost child, unable to find a solid identity in relation to her parents.

Birth order and gender help determine how the character of each child will be molded for the family story. Sibling relationships, or the lack thereof, also become foundational for each child's way of dealing with the complexities of peer relationships later in life. For example, when brothers and sisters fight constantly in childhood, each will carry this expectation of conflict into later peer relationships. One researcher put it this way: "Siblings are often the first partners in life, the first 'marriages' where primary intimacy can be learned."[4]

Temperament of the child. Trying to figure out which of our characteristics are innate and which are shaped by others as we grow is an extremely difficult task. There always is an interplay between the two. We see an innate behavior manifested in our child. Immediately we assign an interpretation to it, because it reminds us of characteristics we've known before. Still, certain characteristics, evident from birth, are worth noting.

First is the level of anxiety. Certain people appear to be fearless, beginning in infancy. Their nervous system seems to be wired in such a way as to preclude apprehension. This trait follows them throughout childhood. Other children are prone to anxiety. These infants may grow into adults who are timid and shy.

Second is the level of friendliness. Some people are slow to warm up to others, seemingly overwhelmed by new experiences and people. As children they are labeled timid and shy. As adults they are the classic introverts (although many people who were timid as children grow up to overcome this). Unfortunately for these children, the American culture demands a certain level of gregarious extroversion, and those wired to be more timid tend to be looked down on.

Third is the degree of eagerness for novel experiences. Some children are willing to plow headlong into any new experience. Others shy away from such experiences and tend to choose the safer route.

Fortunately, we now know that the brain and its neural circuitry are pliable. Even if born fearful, an infant is not automatically condemned to grow into a timid adult. The final results will largely depend on how parents handle their timid child. Many parents instinctively protect their timid infant; unfortunately, this produces an effect opposite of what they intended—a more timid child. Children who are given gentle pressure to be more outgoing tend to lose their timidity by kindergarten.[5]

Maturity of the parents. The more mature and comfortable parents are when their children arrive on the scene, the more likely those parents will be to let their children develop into the characters God intended each to be.

One process that operates in certain families is *splitting.* This process is more characteristic of parents who are less mature and therefore have more unresolved issues lurking in their own past stories. Often where strong favoritism is shown toward one child (followed inevitably by intense sibling rivalry), this process is unfolding. One child reflects the parents' good feelings about themselves, while another child reflects the bad feelings, becoming the black sheep of the family. I have seen this process at work in twins, where one twin is the "good" child and the other is the "bad" one.

I once saw a family who were extremely bright and intellectual. Both parents were Ph.D.s. The two oldest children had gone to prestigious Ivy League schools and, like their parents, were very cerebral. Then the youngest, a boy, came along. This child didn't like intellectual pursuits. He was into drama. He loved to organize the neighborhood into productions in which he played the lead. He hated reading books.

Of course neither parent could identify with these characteristics. Neither of them understood or valued their youngest son's traits. They were writing a family story centered on characters who were intellectual, abstract thinkers who would probably become scholars. As the boy grew, the parents tried hard to suppress his thespian aspirations and direct him into more "productive" pursuits, which for them meant "left-brained" intellectual arenas.

Given his parents' proclivities, how could this boy have come along and developed into a drama person? I think it was because the "right-brained" feeling-over-thinking traits had been lost to both parents, who cherished only intellectual pursuits. In other words, this boy was reflecting a part of both parents that they had denied and suppressed. The parents were saying in effect, *We're not allowed to be into drama, but son, you can be.* Unfortunately, tacked onto the end of that message was *And we'll misunderstand you and fight you all the way.*

The struggle had continued for years, with the boy always feeling inadequate and strange, the parents feeling as though they were doing a bad job. When I finally saw the family, the boy was a teenager ready for college. The parents had been chronically disappointed with this boy. The boy felt inadequate. "I just don't fit in," he said of his family. It was true. The family story didn't seem to have a part for his character.

So then, I have a self that has been refashioned away from the original self God created. This refashioned self has various aspects. Relationships with others, and our participation in the stories that those relationships entail, draw out various aspects of myself. My character changes periodically to meet the demands of the current unfolding story. The way we see others seeing us greatly influences how we see ourselves and which parts of ourselves we display.

One social researcher, Bill Wilmot, summed up the process along these lines:

1. You enter a situation with various parts and roles tucked away in your storehouse.

2. The way you act is experienced by others. They interpret your behavior a certain way, and act accordingly.

3. In turn, you note their behavior and interpret it.

4. You view yourself as you think others do, based on the meaning you assign to their behavior.

5. You revise your sense of self based on what you thought you were, going into the situation, and the new way you think the others perceived you to be.[6]

Roles

The various aspects of my self, pulled out in various situations, become stylized into particular roles that I play. A role is merely the stylized character I play in a given story, an expression of my identity.

We all know that we play certain roles in certain situations: I play the role of Christian psychologist at work, of husband and father at home, and so on. But different stories demand different roles from us. And from the time we are born, it is as though we are handed scripts that carefully delineate which roles we are to play in our family story. We then take these roles with us into the rest of our lives and

continue to play them. Rarely do we realize what is happening and seek
to alter the process. Unfortunately, we often replay our original family
role in the new family story we create. We also assume the same
"emotional position" in our new family story. If you felt victimized by
screaming parents then, you feel victimized by screaming children now.
If you were left out then, you feel left out now, and so on.

The ideal expression of our identity would be the character as it
was originally fashioned by God, with all the gifts, talents, abilities
and propensities operating in harmony with each other, performed in
obedience to him. Unfortunately, we all fall short of this ideal, so
instead we take on the roles we find ourselves playing in the various
stories that surround our lives.

There are any number of roles that we can play in life, each of which
has its roots in the unfolding family story. Let's look briefly at several
of the roles.

☐ The family hero does everything just right, winning undying praise
and adulation from everyone.

☐ The family rebel is constantly in and out of trouble, earning scorn
from everyone.

☐ The family healer is supposedly charged with almost magical
powers to heal the woundedness of various family members.

☐ The lost child somehow gets lost in the shuffle because she never
quite verbalizes her own needs.

☐ Dad's surrogate wife is charged with meeting Dad's emotional
and/or physical needs because his real spouse, for whatever reason, is
unavailable. Mom's surrogate husband functions similarly.

☐ The family mascot says lots of cute things, especially at tense
moments, to defuse anxiety and distract the family from conflict.

The list can go on and on: the athlete, Mom's (or Dad's) best friend,
the mechanic, the intellectual, and so on.

Unfortunately, once we have fallen into a role, it becomes very
difficult to extract ourselves. When people return after twenty, thirty
or forty years to a high-school reunion, it's remarkable how quickly
they fall into the same roles they played so many years before. When

families congregate for special occasions, each member quickly falls into his or her role (the hero tells of his latest exploits, the rebel delineates in gory detail his latest infractions, the mascot entertains, and the like).

Often the various characters in family stories are placed in roles that are in direct opposition to one another. One sibling is the Mother Teresa of the family, ministering to everyone. Set against her role is her brother's; he is the out-of-control rebel who breaks every law and cares only for himself. This can especially be seen in twins, where one twin exhibits one distinct role (such as the much-praised overachiever) and the other the exact opposite (the ne'er-do-well underachiever).

To carry this one step further, some families even divide the children up three ways (provided there are three), one child taking a role that seems basically impulsive and instinctual (childish, naive, carefree), another keeping his feet firmly planted in reality (rational, mature) and a third representing the conscience of the family (principled and moralistic). Table 4 shows how these three character roles can play off each other in any given family.

Child of instinct	Child of reality	Child of conscience
Spontaneous	Deliberate	Rigid
Juvenile	Adult	Paternalistic
Passionate	Reasonable	Principled
Defiant	Traditional	Devoted
Insatiable	Satisfied	Spartan/austere
Uncomplicated	Astute	Wise
Unexamined	Self-aware	Overexamined
Selfish	Empathetic	Self-sacrificing

Table 4. Offsetting sibling roles

Of course any given person could exhibit any one of these traits in different situations. But in many families (especially those that struggle the most with problems) roles often become fixed, and the various players in the story have great difficulty breaking free of their role designations.

Sometimes roles are passed on from one family member to another, especially when the family story still desperately needs the lost character. This is often accomplished at or after funerals, after an important character has died (although it may also happen when one person decides it is time, for whatever reason, to lay aside her role in the family story). A death and funeral may be the single most important event in the unfolding family story. Reconciliations occur as well as emotional banishments. Often the script that informed the deceased person's role is unconsciously handed to another family member: *Here, now you will assume this role. Play it well.*

Sanctification

Sanctification is the process whereby the gap between who God originally made me to be (my original self) and what I in fact became (the refashioned self) is gradually closed. I now begin to express more fully my God-given identity with its gifts, talents and propensities. This, of course, implies choice. I am not frozen into character sketches and roles, hopelessly doomed to fulfill what parents set in motion. I can change!

God renames us. The process of sanctification begins as God gives me a new name. Again, I think the best example of this in the Bible is the story of Jacob. As noted above, when he is born he's the second fraternal twin, born clutching the heel of his brother. His parents see this behavior, name him Jacob (the supplanter, the cheat, the liar) and then expect him to live up to these expectations.

Jacob of course doesn't disappoint his parents' expectations of him. As the family story unfolds, he cheats his brother and flees to his uncle. Thereupon he and his uncle set about to see who can cheat the other most successfully (Laban was as big a cheat as Jacob was).

Then God finally catches up with our hero, the cheat and liar. God gets hold of Jacob's life, and the first thing God does is give him a new name. "Your name will no longer be Jacob [the cheat], but Israel [he struggles with God], because you have struggled with God and with men and have overcome" (Gen 32:28). God sees what Jacob really is and has become, and gives him a new name with all the expectations attached.

Character changes. As God renames us, he expects new behavior and attitudes from us. As these begin to change, our character changes. My entire life becomes a calling from him.

Johnny Cash, well-known country singer, tells his story this way.[7]

> I got a lot of really good stuff from my parents. I'm steeped in the tradition of my father. I even got my family tree going back to 1667, when the first Cash came from Scotland. A lot of my father is in my songs—American tales he told me about riding the freight trains looking for work back in the '20s. Stories my father related to me when I was too young to remember things—the Mississippi flood, the cotton crops. I wrote songs like "Ridin' on the Cottonbelt," a railroad line I was born near. He gave me a lot.

Cash rose in the entertainment world but slowly sank into alcohol and drug use.

> I was on amphetamines. I'd been up five, six nights without sleep and hadn't eaten. My wife was divorcing me. I was in really bad shape. I wasn't getting along with June. I went down to this friend who lived out in the country, near Chattanooga, to hide out. Nearby is the Nickajack Cave. It goes for miles. I drove my Jeep there one night. Had my flashlight. The place was flooded with moonlight at the entrance.
>
> With my flashlight, I went walking in this cave. I knew I was going as far into this cave as I could until the flashlight burned out. When it finally went out, I lay down and gave up. I thought, "Surely my heart must have worn out by now, so I'll just lay here and die." I had no strength. I had no idea how long I'd been walking and crawling to get where I was.
>
> Then I felt something—that love, the warm presence of God that I knew as a boy. I understood that I wasn't going to die, there were still things I had to do. "But how can I? I don't know how to get out of here! I got no light." Then the voice seemed to answer back,

"Get up and go."

I was sweating. I got up in the pitch darkness and felt the air moving against me, and I knew the way the air was going had to be the way out. Everything was beautiful and good. I drove all the way back to Nashville.

Cash's struggle for sobriety and a "new name" continued for a number of years. He has not abused alcohol since the mid-1980s. He gives the credit for this to God.

Role changes. As our character changes, the roles we have assumed in the numerous stories we inhabit (family, occupation, school, church, community) also change. Paul is an excellent example of this. When Christ confronts him on the road to Damascus, his life is changed. When his life changes, his role in society immediately changes. He turns immediately from persecutor of the church to defender and enlarger of the church. We are not told how his roles changed in other ways, but we can speculate that family roles changed, his role on the council changed and probably his role as a tentmaker changed in some way.

Story changes. When characters in a story change, the story must change. No longer can the plot unfold in its predictable manner. When God changes our name, and our character and roles change, the stories in which we live also begin to change. This begins with our family story.

Conforming to God's Story. I've been intrigued by the story of Jabez found in the book of 1 Chronicles. Just two verses in the fourth chapter (vv. 9-10) describe his life. First we learn he's more honorable than his brothers. Then we learn of his background. His mother had named him Jabez, which seems to mean "sorrow bringer" or "painful one." She did this evidently because he had brought pain to her (possibly the pain of childbirth, or her husband ran off when he was born). At any rate, with this name she described him and predicted what she thought he would become. *He brought me pain. He'll just continue to bring others pain too.*

But Jabez was not content to live out the character his mother had hung on him. Having "cried out to God," Jabez rose above the "sorrow bringer" label his mother had given him and became the one who was honored above his brothers.

Exercise. Questions to write, discuss with a friend or think through on your own.

1. Think of the name you were given at birth. Who named you? Why do you think you were given that name?

2. What do you think your mother's hopes, desires and expectations were for you when you were growing up? your father's? How were these communicated to you?

3. Think of yourself in relation to each of your brothers and sisters. How did each respond to you?

4. Now think of and list the role(s) you assumed. If you want, you can expand this question to describe how you actually played each role out.

5. Now think of your conversion experience. Explain what that experience was like for you. Can you discern a new name that God gave you? What character changes have come about since that time? What still needs to change?

Exercise. If you are a parent, you can make this a whole family project. Or you can do this exercise alone, again based on the family story in which you developed.

1. Get a large sheet of newsprint. Each person in the family is to take a section of the newsprint and draw a picture of him- or herself. After this is done, each family member will write under his or her picture a list of the particular parts of self that are represented. You can mix brief descriptions with celebrity names that reflect these parts. Your lists could look something like this:

Dad's list	Mom's list	Junior's list
John Wayne	Kermit the Frog	Robin Williams
Mother Teresa	Mary Tyler Moore	Albert Einstein
Thomas Edison	Doubting Thomas	Chance taker
Fixer of everything	Maid	Bo Jackson

Every family member should share his or her list with every other
family member. Have each member now tell when each part emerges
("I'm Robin Williams at the dinner table"). Then say whether or not
that part is liked. Discuss how the different parts of each person get
along or don't get along with other parts ("My John Wayne does get
along with your Kermit the Frog very well").

2. Now have each family member draw a picture of every other
family member (pets can be included too), and again go around and
describe the different character aspects of each person. Each person,
in describing other family members, should attempt to be positive.

5

The
Story's
Premise

W<i>hat made the Simmons</i> family tick? What was the principlc around which the family seemed to be organized? What in fact was their family story all about? This seemed hard to discern amid all the verbiage about young Billy's problems with the law, about Julie's perfections and Marie's shortcomings.

Ferreting out the central issues from the cacophony of voices straining to be heard is often my hardest task in counseling. But I realized that the premise of this family would be the central issue that set this family story in the particular direction that it took.

As I continued to work with the Simmons family, I learned of Bill's striving for acceptance and Mary's yearning for affirmation and a sense of competence, and how these differing premises had drawn them into conflict. I learned that the Simmons family premise seemed to bounce over the years between these two premises—acceptance and competence. Julie seemed to embody the competence theme and to have performed quite well under its dictates. Marie leaned more toward the premise of acceptance and had longed for that sense of belonging. Young Billy was harder to read, seemingly gravitating toward acceptance, then competence as a premise for his life story.

The Power of Premises

Your family story, like all other stories, has a premise. What was the underlying premise(s) of your family as you grew up? What about the premise(s) in your current family? How were these premises worked out practically in the overall story development within the family?

So what's a premise? For an author writing a story, the premise is the one-line explanation of what the story is about and what happens to the characters in the story as a result of the core conflict. Often in story writing the premise is expressed in terms like these: "Greed *leads to* disgrace," or "Love *leads to* a happy life."

The premise acts as a chisel, shaping the raw material of the family story and each family member. Once established, the premise, for better or worse, keeps the family focused. The premise includes the family's shared approach to daily living (attitudes lived out in behavior).

Wait a minute, you may be thinking; *my family had no premise. We just went about living. Father worked for IBM. Mom stayed home and raised us. My older brother is a lawyer. I'm a bricklayer. That's it for my family, and growing up.*

But if you've followed me thus far and agree that you yourself and your family have a particular story, it stands to reason that these stories have a particular premise. Think back to Bill and Mary Simmons. In Bill's family of origin the premise was *acceptance.* Either directly or indirectly, the story that unfolded in this family involved this premise. For Mary's family the premise was *competence,* and again, the story as it unfolded directly pointed to this premise.

In my own family, as I was growing up, the central premise was acceptance. This premise was constantly underscored, especially by my mother. "What will people think?" was a critical question she would ask. Our family story, and the way it was written, was always colored by this particular premise.

There was a good side to this premise (there are good and bad aspects to any family premise). The acceptance premise made me very sensitive to other people. As a result, through the years I have had many friends who have been very important to me. I think this premise has made me a good counselor, able to attend to the needs of those who come for help.

But unfortunately, there was also a negative side to this premise. In any activity, I have tended to reflect on the effect the activity will have on others *(they like me, they accept me)* rather than on the inherent goodness or appropriateness of the activity. The tendency is to "play to the audience," attempting to please everyone.

Was the premise in your family basically constructive or destructive? I realize I've just said that every premise has both a positive and a negative side. And it will be vital for you to see, even in the most negative premises, that positive outcomes have come (or should have come) from them, depending on our response. But for now, consider your *initial reaction* to the premise that was operating in your family. Was the premise presented in ways that were constructive and positive for you, enhancing your sense of yourself and your ability to live productively? Or was the premise primarily negative, leading you to doubt yourself and stumble through life?

Constructive premises are optimistic, active, open. Premises that are basically positive will help the characters in the family story to

- ☐ feel good about themselves
- ☐ function well independently or in cooperation
- ☐ feel free to speak clearly, directly and honestly
- ☐ disagree and have conflict, yet feel safe and cared for
- ☐ participate in community as well as family activities
- ☐ have a zest for life
- ☐ have a confident, hopeful outlook
- ☐ display resourcefulness, a creative attitude in problem-solving
- ☐ take risks and make changes

Destructive premises, on the other hand, are pessimistic, passive, closed. These are evident if your family is marked by the following:

- ☐ frozenness or flatness; lack of interest and energy
- ☐ anxiety, doubts, fear *(life is dangerous)*
- ☐ sense of limitation or helplessness

☐ rigidity, strong need for control, unwillingness to alter the status quo
☐ feeling bad about yourself
☐ too much dependence on each other, and/or inability to cooperate
☐ indirect and unclear communication; keeping secrets
☐ avoidance of conflict, or frequent unresolved conflict
☐ isolation from the world beyond the family

Did your family premise seem to render family members active ("We Smiths can do anything we set out to do") or passive ("Be careful—people will always do you wrong")?

The premise limits your perspectives and responses but also enables you to live more predictably. Unfortunately, living predictably is not the same as living biblically. Limiting perspectives, in the experiences you face, means that certain issues are filtered out while others are highlighted. Have you ever noticed how several people looking at virtually the same situation can come to radically different conclusions? That's because we all wear a "pair of glasses" that filters our experiences so that we can make interpretations and draw conclusions. We do it constantly and effortlessly. The process has to go on, but we need to be aware of it. Usually it takes others who are close to us to point out that we are focusing on certain issues to the exclusion of others.

I once heard of a minister who decided to go back through fourteen years of his sermons to get the gist of each. He was astonished to find that almost everyone had the theme "Try to . . .":

"Try to witness more."
"Try to be faithful."
"Try to give more."
"Try to build community."

Without his awareness, his premise ("competence equals working hard") had seeped into everything he said to his congregation. Grace was almost completely absent from his sermons.

Once a family's premise is established, everything that happens in the family seems to further that premise. It's not easy to discard faulty premises. The family keeps struggling under the old premise even though the story seems not to work. Premises are rarely if ever scrutinized.

Personal Story Premises

Not only your family story but also your personal story has a premise. As with the family story premise, our personal story premises are rarely taken out and scrutinized. We just live them out. Remember what was said in the previous chapter about the formation of your character. You're created by God a certain way. Your parents shape you into a character that retains some of what God created you to be, but eliminates some elements and adds others.

Your parents were shaping your character in accordance with the story premise that existed in their minds. *This family story is about acceptance. We need a character who will be very lovable and accepting to everyone. Someone who is nonconfrontational, noncom petitive, always compliant and giving. Here's our new son Jimmy. We will now mold him according to our family premise. As he enters our family story, he will be a very nice, acceptable boy.*

The family premise is driving the family story as Jimmy enters. Jimmy's personal story premise will follow closely the premise of the family story. In some cases personal and family premises appear to be identical. But there can also be vast variations between the family premise and the individual premise, especially as the individual matures and continues to write his or her own story apart from the family-of-origin story.

From your personal premise, your character was developed, and the role(s) you played in your family story was forged, perhaps along one of these lines:

☐ "Lad of infinite promise" (competence)

☐ "Troublemaker" (control)

☐ "Miss nice girl" (acceptance)

I have found that a few core premises are influential in the majority of families and individuals. Each of these can have a constructive slant or a destructive slant, depending on the individual or family story involved.

Acceptance

Acceptance means approval, favor, recognition, sanction, endorsement. The premise of acceptance builds people who are focused outward toward others, who have genuine concern for others and tend to monitor others for even the smallest clues of acceptance or rejection. This, I believe, has been the premise of my personal story and that of my family of origin.

On the constructive side, this premise works to create *an overriding feeling of harmony and peace within the family.* Many who view this family from the outside or are invited in to participate with it are struck by a sense that it provides a haven of blessing and of peace. As you were growing up, if you especially liked to visit the house of certain friends, the premise of their family story was probably acceptance. It was in such families that you found the warmest welcome and the greatest hospitality.

The acceptance premise also fosters *a genuine concern for others, leading to an emphasis on the struggles and needs of others.* The acceptance premise also builds people who are very sensitive to others, who stand ready to serve others, who will be loyal to friends:

☐ I must take seriously the concerns of others.

☐ Being of service to others is a priority in my life.

The destructive angle, however, leads family members to think, *I must be acceptable to everybody. Being rejected leads to abandonment and death.* Taken negatively, the acceptance premise builds people who are overly compliant and self-effacing, people who will go along with the crowd in any situation as long as they are not rejected. Here are some core beliefs that go with this negative slant:

☐ You're nothing unless you're loved.

☐ You need to be understood.

☐ To be rejected is the worst thing in the world.

☐ You have to please others.

☐ You can't be alone.

Mark, a thirty-two-year-old social worker, grew up in a family whose story premise was acceptance. His comments exemplify the negative slant that this premise can take:

> Someday, just once I'd like to have a relationship with someone I don't have to focus on pleasing. It really reaches ridiculous proportions. I have to please my parents, my wife, my boss and all my coworkers of course. But it gets even worse than that. When an appliance breaks and needs to be taken back to the store, I can't do it. I just can't see myself hurting the clerk. So my wife has to take it back. I get a sick feeling in my stomach if anyone—paper boy, gas-station attendant, *anyone*—is ever in the least bit angry with me.

Competence

Competence includes the concepts of ability, expertise, mastery, skill. Competence-premise families see their children go off to Ivy League schools, receive scholarships, excel in sports and reach the highest levels of corporate and political life. These are the families whose vans sport bumper stickers that say, "I have an honor student at Frost Elementary School." The walls of their homes and offices display the diplomas, the Phi Beta Kappa certificates—all the marks of success. Their conversations will turn quickly to areas of competence.

The constructive angle of this premise is the conviction that *doing tasks honestly and thoroughly leads to success.* These families demonstrate that a task worth doing is worth doing right. They expect the highest performance from their members, and outsiders can see the results of jobs done well. The competence premise pushes people to the highest rungs of achievement. Members of these families excel in many walks of life and become the leaders in society.

Taken negatively, this premise leaves people with the feeling that nothing's enough. They work and work to attain the highest levels, but somehow they never feel as though they've quite made it. So they keep on pushing, keep on working those eighty-hour weeks, hoping this time to achieve a sense of final accomplishment, but that feeling never seems to come.

The negative angle for this premise is the feeling that *love is based on performance, and I can't ever seem to do quite well enough to get the love I need.* Children in these families receive the message *I'll love you if you do well on this test or project, or in this athletic endeavor.* They grow up with the following beliefs:

☐ You are what you accomplish.

☐ Success is everything.

☐ There are winners and losers in life.

☐ I have to be best at whatever I do.

☐ If you make a mistake you'll fail, and failure is the end of the world.

"My father was the type who couldn't express love—only approval or disapproval," Judy, a forty-three-year-old woman, related.

Once I got a B on a report card, and he said, "'What's this?" I said, "Why don't you say anything about all the A's?" He said, "I expect that. I expect you to be perfect." The good news is that he trained me to be extremely capable, so I am very successful—I can take care of myself. The downside is that I'm a driven workaholic. I can't make a mistake, and I'm always walking on eggs. One false move, and it's all undone. I feel as if I'm only as good as my last accomplishment.[1]

Control

Other words for control are *mastery, initiation, responsibility.* Control-premise families initiate much of the action that takes place in the world. They lead many of the work groups in businesses and organizations.

Taken positively, the control premise fosters the belief that *I must take responsibility and initiate action.* These families take a great deal of responsibility in finding out what needs to be done in a given situation, then initiating actions and leading others to realize goals that are beneficial to an organization. The best aspects of leadership are found here.

Taken negatively, the control premise states, *I must be in control. It is too threatening for me to follow.* When this issue shades over into the negative, a family may teach its members the following:

☐ We never get sick.

☐ The world is a threatening place.

☐ You're the only one who can solve your problems.

☐ Others are trying to control you.

☐ Rules and regulations imprison you.

☐ If a person gets too close, they'll control you.

When a family's control premise works negatively, members tend to hang back and be generally suspicious. One man, now in his fifties, described his family this way:

> My parents led a very circumscribed life and raised us to do the same. They told us that the FBI had a file on all of us and that once they got your fingerprints, they kept the file running, so you'd better never screw up. My parents always played it very, very safe: They said, "Don't make waves. Don't call attention to yourself. Stay out of trouble."[2]

Survival

The message here is *survive, don't make waves, rely on yourself.* The people with the survival premise come from the most disorganized families. These are the families with alcoholic members, or severely abusive parents, or parents who are never around, leaving the kids to fend for themselves. Parents don't parent much in these families. Children learn from an early age that if they are to survive and thrive, they will have to do it on their own. People just aren't going to be there to give much help.

The good news for many of these children growing up in survival families is they often grow up to be extremely competent. They have had to learn early to take responsibility themselves and learn the tasks of living. The bad news is that these children lack a sense of nurture and wholeness. They tend to think that something is missing and incomplete in themselves. There's this persistent feeling that if they'd been better people, they would not have received the rough treatment that they got growing up. So, unfortunately, there's a feeling of badness wedded to their competence.

Trust, obviously, is a major problem that tends to plague these folks most of their lives. The people closest to them have tended to let them down, so why get close?

In the worst case senarios, survival-premise kids grow up to live on the margins of society and parent badly. Fortunately, many of these kids grow up to make some of the most significant contributions to our society; their motivation growing out of the deprivation they experienced as children.

Premise	Description	Plus	Minus
Acceptance	Be loved; please others; don't be alone	Service; attend to people	Overly compliant; self-effacing
Competence	Love = performance-based; winners/losers	High achievement	Nothing is enough
Control	World = threat; people too close control you	Leadership; vigilance	Feel vulnerable; overly controlling
Survival	I must take care of myself to live	Self-reliant; discern-ing; responsible	Lack of trust; trouble with relationships

The Premises Side by Side

If three people of these three different premises were playing golf together, the competence-premise person would be trying to win, the control-premise person would be making sure everyone played by the rules, and the acceptance-premise person would be trying to strike up a conversation at every opportunity.

Possibly the "ideal premise" would combine elements of each of these—acceptance, competence, control—producing a loving, accepting family that is not overcontrolling but able to take leadership positions and keep achievement goals in perspective. The children from such a family would tend to be independent, outgoing, active, assertive and tolerant and would have high levels of self-esteem.

Changing the Premise

Stories change as premises are changed. That's right—your personal premise and your family premise are not set in concrete! Quite the contrary. Now it's time to change your family story's premise and your personal premise.

Remember, every premise has a positive and a negative spin. Your initial response to your family premise may have been negative. But even the most negative premises contain positive elements. As you reflect back on the family premise in your family of origin, begin to consider what God may have been doing in that situation, painful and traumatic though it may have been.

A woman was raised in a family whose premise was control. Everything she did was monitored, directed, evaluated and criticized. She could never do anything right. As she reflected on her premise, at first she could see only the negative in this. But then she began to realize that she had an eye for detail that was often helpful in her work. She was also able to monitor the concerns of her children in ways that were helpful to them.

The first step in changing your personal and family premise(s) is to note what these are. Then you need to tease out what has been positive and what has been negative about these premises. Here's an exercise to help.

Exercise. Make two lists with the following headings, and fill them in as completely as possible.

Individual premise(s)

Positive aspects	Negative aspects

Family of origin premise(s)

Positive aspects	Negative aspects

Current family premise(s)

Positive aspects	Negative aspects

If you are married, show your list to your spouse, and encourage him or her to make a list also. Now compare lists. Discuss with each other how your current premise(s) are helping and/or hurting each other and other family members.

If you are not married, make the above lists, but share them with a friend or a small group. Set goals for yourself: how can you change the negative aspects of your existing premise(s)?

6
The Story's Plot

How *was I to make* sense of the Simmons family? Here was a couple attempting to scrve God and humankind, who had become hopelessly mired down in petty squabbles, whose only son was a felon, whose daughter had already given birth to a baby out of wedlock.

In some ways the Simmons story resembled the parable Jesus told of the prodigal son, though at the moment Billy had not come to his senses and begged forgiveness of his father. In other ways the story resembled the story of the good Samaritan, with Bill and Mary selflessly giving of themselves to help the down and out. And Julie and Marie added their own twists and subplots to the story.

You could unfold the plot of each individual in the family story separately—"Bill's Story," "Mary's Story," "Julie's Story," "Marie's Story" and "Billy's Story." Marie's story appeared to be a tragedy, of potential given and then wasted. Billy seemed to be writing an action-adventure thriller. Julie's story seemed to be a charming romance. Bill and Mary could have seen elements of all these plots in their own unfolding story.

As noted in the previous chapter, each family story has a particular premise. A cast of characters is present. Now the story starts to unfold.

The characters begin to act and interact, and presto, the action explodes. The working out of the premise—the unfolding of the story, the course of action that the story involves—is the plot of that family story. Plot involves action. Action always involves conflict. One way to look at plot is to see it as the history of a conflict.

Elements of Plot

A good plot involves several elements:

1. There was a likable hero (you, the *protagonist*),

2. who had reason to set out on a journey (your *mission* in life, which provides you with a particular *intention*),

3. when a threat occurred (*complications* arise, leading to *conflict*),

4. from which there was hopefully a hero-inspired way out,

5. which resulted in a safe return and ultimately a happy ending.

Hero. Like it or not, you are the hero of your personal story. (I know what you're thinking: *I don't feel much like a hero.*) Whether heroic feelings arise or not, the simple fact is that each personal story needs a hero. And no one else can fill that bill. You could also say that you're the hero of your family story. That's because you tend to see this story unfolding with you as the protagonist and all other family characters lining up around you.

Motivation. Motivation is that which incites us to action. It's the incentive to do anything. All characters in a story must have motivation, be it money, life, love, self-esteem, love of truth or something else. As Christians, we would all like to think that our motives are basically pure. Yet as I consider my own motives for pursuing the important things in my life—vocation, acts of charity, vital relationships—I find them often hopelessly mixed with impurities. Fortunately, God can redeem our motives (Phil 1:15-18).

It is important to examine our motives, to attempt to see just why it is that we do what we do. Accountability is most helpful here. Frankly, I do not trust my motives. I realize that I often act, then rationalize a perfectly good motive for acting that way, when in fact my heart has been impure. Being able to spread my motives out for inspection by another responsible person is critical for me.

I would like to think that my motive in counseling people is to help them get through suffering and difficulties and find peace and fulfillment. And this *is* one motive I have for being a psychologist. But when I dig deeper into my heart, I find that I like it when people come to me seeking advice; it makes me feel important and valued. I also like to be paid. And I like the title "Dr." in front of my name. That sounds prestigious.

Once motivated, the hero needs to have an intention in mind, a plan to accomplish whatever is important to him or her. Many people have a very ill-defined sense of what they intend to achieve over their lifetime. With no burning sense of what truly is important to them, and few if any goals, they stumble through life from incident to incident. As a result, their life's story seems to lack meaning.

Exercise. If you are uncertain of your motivations and don't have a good sense of your destination, the following questions should be helpful.

1. Determine what things are the strongest motivators in your life (love, fame, riches, integrity, respect, relationships, etc.), and list these in your journal. With someone you trust and respect, evaluate your list for accuracy *(are these really my motivations?)* and validity *(should these be my motivations?).*

2. Determine your destination. Your destination has two elements:

☐ *Who I want to be.* First think of those character traits you want most to develop. Make a list of these, adding a brief evaluation of how far along you are in achieving each.

☐ *What I want to do.* Now list the particular things that you wish to achieve. Your list can include short-term and long-term accomplishments.

3. Begin to formulate a plan for how you will reach your destination. Regardless of the shape of your plan, you will probably want to include specific activities, habits or relationships that will be helpful in achieving your goals.

Quest. Based on motivation and intention, a quest is initiated. *I must now go into the world to* . . . make a million bucks, become the greatest evangelist since Billy Graham, be the best mother that eight children ever saw, build the tallest skyscrapers, be loved and adored by millions of people, etc., etc.

Pastor Walt Gerber recalled how a man whose company was on the Fortune 500 list and who had a personal worth in excess of $500 million came into his office and said, "I climbed the ladder to the top, and found it was resting on the wrong building." Jesus spoke of precisely such a failed quest in Luke 12:13-21.

The Christian's quest should begin with a sense of call, which is in fact our vocation. The Christian sense of calling is by God, for God and to God (1 Pet 2:9). The church then is a gathering of the called, and in that sense it is a vocational institution.[1]

So my primary calling is to be God's servant in the world, living in faith and obedience. My calling should take precedence over any occupational, recreational or relational pursuit. Unfortunately, many people—men in particular—let their occupation take precedence over their vocation. Others permit relationships to take precedence over vocation.

One woman I know has turned down a number of offers of marriage because she believes God's claim on her life involves becoming an overseas missionary. She has not ruled out marriage, but she knows God will have to bring into her life a man who will not distract her from her primary vocation.

Our call, once established, should then shape our character, our roles, our story premise and the unfolding plot. Call should be that basic and foundational to our stories. Call will shape character as I live out the fact that I am a child of God. Call will shape premise since my story is about being called to God—acceptable to him, controlled by him, competent to serve him. Call shapes the unfolding plot because however the story unfolds, I live my life to God's glory.

Once this priority is straight, we can go out into the world and meet God and serve him in our work. In this sense our work can become a sacrament (a visible sign of an invisible reality, where the ordinary points to the supernatural). Now I can approach my workbench, my desk, my garage, my dirty laundry on Monday morning in faith, knowing that as I work at these tasks, I in fact do it for the Lord.

Antagonists

Our lives are filled with characters. Characters within the family, of course, directly affect our unfolding stories when we are young. As we grow, more characters from the outside enter our stage and play parts in our unfolding stories.

As we look back, we can remember and name many of the characters who were important to us. I can still recall a number of children who lived in the Arlington, Virginia, neighborhood where I grew up. There were the Sharp sisters down the street, one a year older, the other a year younger than I. We played together for hours, and I began to learn something of the ways of females from them. Across the creek were the Detwilers. Steve was closest in age to me. His father, a physician, owned a large piece of land on which the whole neighborhood would assemble on long, hot summer evenings to play Capture the Flag. Steve had a way of pinning me to the ground and not letting me up until I said something demeaning about myself.

As I ventured off to school, my cast of characters expanded, now including adults in the role of authorities over me. Teachers began to take an active part in my unfolding story, as did Sunday-school teachers and youth workers. There were Mrs. McGinnis, Mrs. Cunningham and Mrs. Powell, who were my first-, second- and third-grade teachers. I think the elementary teacher who had the most positive effect on me was Mr. Fields, my sixth-grade teacher. He was the first man I had as a teacher. He served as a male role model I could look up to. I worked hard for him and completed several complicated assignments for which I was highly praised.

As we begin our quest, inevitably there arises an antagonist, someone or something that is pushing in the opposite direction of our goals. These antagonists can be somewhat benign or very forceful and belligerent. They become significant characters in our story.

My seventh-grade shop teacher was one of the most trying people I had to deal with as I was growing up. I can't remember his name. He threw my project in the trash in front of the class and presented me with a serious complication that went unresolved for fourteen years (I explain the story in fuller detail below).

Exercise. Take a few moments to list the most significant characters, both positive and negative, who have been in your life. Note when they were prominent in your story and the net effects of their influence on your unfolding story.

Character	Time/circumstance	Effect on your story

Antagonists have an amazing way of hanging around for years, at least in our minds. They inhabit our stories even long after they are dead. Unfortunately, as they continue to inhabit our minds, they also continue to use up our energy supplies, inevitably in very negative ways. "I can't believe he did that to me," a woman intones about her extremely abusive father, now dead for over twenty years. A man cannot forgive his wife for walking out on him seven years ago. The painful memories persist. But memories of this nature are not just static photographs of past events. Researchers have found that a memory brings emotions with it. Each time we bring up a memory it's as if we relive events (positive and negative) with all the feelings attached.

Set this book down for a moment, and let your mind wander back to when you were little. Imagine for a moment the frustrations that plagued you—a taunting older brother, a critical mother—and note how this left you feeling. Now think of the issues that lay behind these frustrations. (For example, "My brother taunted me. I felt inadequate. My mother was critical of me. Love was always conditional.") Compare these frustrations to those that haunt you today. (For example, "I always feel inadequate, even when I do a good job. I feel that no one will love me unless I perform optimally.") You will probably find that the issues remain the same.

How can I free myself of the antagonists that have so haunted my memories? Is there any hope, or am I eternally trapped with the old characters who were a part of my past story?

In the pages ahead, we will look specifically at ways to release the past and redeem the memories. By definition, antagonists bring us into conflict. And conflict with an antagonist is the mix that produces plot.

Conflict: Pushing and Clashing

A story is movement. Someone pushes, someone or something else pushes back. At some level there's always a disagreement; sometimes there's a fight. Strong forces, with differing goals, come together and clash.

Essentially stories involve the history of a conflict. They begin with the realization of the conflict. As the story proceeds, the conflict grows until a climax (the highest point of interest in the story) is reached. Then the conflict is resolved to end the story.

Obviously our unfolding individual and family stories are not that simple. Nor is God's cosmic unfolding Story, which is the story of a long-term conflict between good and evil. But the elements of conflict in our stories are similar whether in literature or in our living room.

We tend to think of conflict as bad, something to be avoided at all costs. This is not necessarily true. In fact, conflict is essential for character development. Family stories involve action and conflict, showing how these conflicts shaped each family member in particular ways. Several types can be listed:

- ☐ to eliminate an opponent
- ☐ to overcome an obstacle

☐ to avert a disaster

Conflict in family stories involves any of several generic forms:

☐ man against man (or woman against woman)

☐ man against men (war)

☐ man against woman

☐ woman or man against nature

☐ man or woman against God

☐ man against himself or woman against herself (two sides of one's nature in conflict)

Exercise. Take a moment and think about the major conflicts that you have experienced over your lifetime. Note what type each conflict was and when it occurred. When you come to the column titled "Resolution," think of how each conflict *changed you.* That is the critical factor in every conflict that enters our lives.

Type of conflict and particular incident	Date(s) occurred	Resolution
Me against God		
Me against men and/or women		
Me against community/ institutions		
Me against nature		
Me against myself		

Conflict, as it arises between family members, can be overt or covert. In overt conflict, people take various stances, many of which are quite unhelpful for conflict resolution. People will generally take a stance according to the role they've assumed in the family story. Their role comes from the character they're given and assume.

Because conflict is often handled poorly, much of it is driven underground. Then there is usually triangling, often between the parents and a child: the child is drawn into the conflict to defuse the tension between the parents. Through triangling the parents can focus their energies on the child (perhaps he is acting up, failing in school, behaving in sexually inappropriate ways) and be distracted from the disagreements that first troubled them.

In *The Seven Habits of Highly Effective People* Stephen Covey gives six paradigms of human interaction:

☐ Win/lose. This is the authoritarian approach: "I must get my way, and you can't get yours." For many of us, this approach is the one most deeply scripted in us since birth. We don't know how to be with each other, even in intimate relationships, without competition. We haven't been taught cooperation, only competition. Competition is the opposite of trusting intimacy. It requires me to be guarded and cautious.

☐ Lose/win. The message here is "Go ahead, have your way with me. . . . I'm a loser. . . . I'll do anything to keep the peace." These are the pleasers and the appeasers. They bury their feelings along with their needs.

☐ Lose/lose. When two win/lose people get together, neither will back down. When one finally loses, he or she will do anything to even the score.

☐ Win. These people don't necessarily want their antagonist to lose. What matters is they get what they want. "I will secure my own needs; it's up to you to secure yours."

☐ Win/win or no deal. If we can't come up with a solution that is agreeable to both of us, we agree to disagree agreeably, and there is no deal. There is no need to manipulate or cajole. "I wouldn't want to get my way and not have you feel good about it. In the end that would erode our relationship."

☐ Win/win. This person constantly seeks mutual benefit for himself and his antagonist. This does not always mean consensus on an issue. That's unrealistic. It does mean that each of us maintains our dignity and integrity while discussing the issue.[2]

Obviously it is the fifth and sixth patterns that produce constructive, cooperative relationships between those engaged in conflict. Remember, the purpose of conflict is not to establish a winner. Ideally, the purpose of conflict is to *understand* the issues and the emotions they evoke.

Exercise. Set the book aside again and answer the following questions.

1. In your family-of-origin story, how was conflict handled?

___ It was avoided.

___ Someone always yielded.

___ Someone always forced his or her own way on everyone else.

___ There was healthy negotiation.

2. In your present family story, how is conflict handled?

3. How do you personally handle conflict?

___ Win/lose

___ Lose/win

___ Lose/lose

___ Win

___ Win/win or no deal

___ Win/win

Complications: The Plot Thickens

Complications arise in our unfolding family story when we intend to do something and our intentions are denied for one reason or another. Actually conflict and complication go hand in hand in storytelling. So most if not all complications involve losses. All of us experience the losses that seem to accompany each and every day. Some of those losses seem rather trivial in hindsight—the loss of minor possessions, the loss of an hour of work, the loss of a scheduled recreational event. Then there are the losses that become complications in the form of overwhelming tragedy or protracted suffering. Those times when we have cried out to God, "Why me?" The greater the loss, the greater the complication. These dramatic complications may weigh us down for years, distracting us from the "normal" unfolding of our stories, draining energy away from us.

One day at a large convention, I ate my lunch in the handicapped section. I was the only person who was not in a wheelchair. As I looked at those people, some of whom undoubtedly had been wheelchair-bound most of their lives, I tried to imagine how this very obvious complication had shaped their lives for better or for worse.

The first great complication in my life came when I was six years old. My mother took me into the woods to dig for worms to feed our pet turtle. Just as we approached the creek, I found a small, rusty pocketknife someone had dropped some time earlier. I picked it up as my mother walked on ahead and found a patch of soft, wet earth to dig in. While she concentrated on digging, I opened the knife and began to whittle a twig. Unfortunately, I didn't know proper knife techniques, and on my second stroke at the stick, I thrust the knife into the pupil of my left eye.

I was rushed to the hospital. An eye specialist was summoned, and he whisked me into surgery. Three stitches were placed directly in my pupil. I spent a week in the hospital. My mother alternated sleeping beside me in my room and praying for my safety in the hospital. (This, of course, was a major complication for my mother also. I don't think she really got over it for the rest of her life.)

The net result was that in my left eye I have only partial vision. I guess I would be considered legally blind in that eye.

As you read this, you likely felt dismayed to imagine this accident happening to a young, exuberant boy with his whole life spread before him. You probably have already deduced that this complication had major, lasting effects on my life.

Interestingly, though, the fact that I see very poorly in my left eye *never* was an issue for me as I grew up. I played sports, even center field in baseball (you'd think depth perception would be a problem there). I got my driver's license without any problem. I started wearing glasses when I was sixteen because of normal vision nearsightedness in my right eye. There was only one time when this complication directly entered into my unfolding story to cause a major shift in direction.

When I was twenty-one, I had just transferred from one school to another. This was in 1968, at the height of the Vietnam War. I immediately received a notice from the draft board informing me that I was 1-A and that I was to report to Richmond for my physical and for induction in the army.

I panicked. My soon-to-be wife Marcy and I were planning to be married in less than a year. I wanted to finish my schooling and get on with a career. Going off to war didn't figure in my plans.

So I boarded a bus at the courthouse early one June morning and headed to Richmond. Like the other young men on the bus, I was extremely apprehensive. I stood all day in my skivvies undergoing various medical tests. Toward the end of the day, the issue of my eye came up. A doctor examined it and immediately ordered me out of line to see a specialist. I was detained in Richmond another day so that my eye could be examined more closely. The result of all this fuss was that I was reclassified 4-F (medical deferment).

In addition to life-altering difficulties, more mundane complications confront us daily. The baby's screams interrupt when we are trying to finish dinner. A traffic jam makes us late to work. A phone call at the office keeps us from completing an important contract. These minor complications distract us and detour us from our intended paths.

All complications, whether mundane or catastrophic, involve suffering. You probably wouldn't say that a minor loss caused you great suffering; nonetheless, there was a degree of suffering. Certainly the major complications involve considerable suffering. Our culture has effectively taught us that all suffering and pain are bad, that if we experience any suffering whatsoever we should move away from it, get rid of it, as quickly as possible.

It's interesting to follow the story of Israel as Moses led the people out of Egypt in the great exodus. Think about it for a minute. It would have been easy simply to lead them north in Egypt and take a quick turn to the east and into the Promised Land. The journey could have taken a few weeks. No problem. But notice how God sets the people up, how he leads them into complications. He backs them up against the Red Sea with the world's mightiest army at their heels. He leads them into a desert with no food or water. Why does God confront them with complications?

I think God realized that he could get the Hebrew people out of Egypt easily. The trick was to get Egypt out of the people. When faced with complications, the people acted like Egyptians. By placing them in the middle of complications, God could show them that ultimately he was their source of life, sustenance, defense, deliverance.

Complications serve a purpose. They may come into our lives to
☐ point up our flaws and shortcomings
☐ give us opportunity to see God's hand at work in our lives (C. S. Lewis noted that while God whispers to us during times of well-being, he shouts at us during times of suffering)
☐ drive us to our knees and make us more dependent on our Creator and Sustainer
☐ help us clarify what is truly important in life
Ultimately these dramatic complications shape us profoundly and point our stories in different directions.

This profound shaping is not automatic, though. In fact, as complications arise, bringing suffering, it seems to me that there are always two possible responses.

1. I am overwhelmed by the complication, feel completely victimized by it, and allow the circumstances of it to dominate my life. This is the classic victim position.

2. I choose to allow the complication and suffering to mold me.

The second alternative is usually not entered into immediately. As a complication arises and envelops us, we are overwhelmed, and for a time we completely lose any broader perspective.

Exercise. Consider several set-pieces in the lives of biblical characters. Note how these dramatic complications drastically changed the life of the character, for good or for ill.
☐ Jacob wrestles with a man (Gen 32:22-32)
☐ Moses kills an Egyptian (Ex 2:11-25)
☐ David sees Bathsheba bathing (2 Sam 11)
☐ Saul (Paul) on the road to Damascus (Acts 9)

I was taking metal shop class in seventh grade. The teacher directed us to make a small metal box. I worked hard on it, though I was not very talented with my hands. The teacher then lined the whole class up, each with project in hand, and opened his gradebook. By turns he looked at our work and wrote down a grade. When he got to me, he took my box, tossed it into the trash in front of the whole class, and marked an F in his gradebook. As I said, I had worked hard on that project. This was a major complication in the unfolding plot of my life.

As an immediate result of this complication, I decided that I was useless with my hands and should never attempt handmade projects. This rule stuck with me on into adult life and marriage, until my wife and I decided to buy a very old house and restore it. We thought, like every amateur who has ever attempted this, that we had planned the right amount of time and help to complete the job. But of course, halfway through the project I ran out of money and had to dismiss the professional help. That meant that I was left to do much of the work our house needed. Armed with my *Reader's Digest* handyman book and my meager tool kit, I set out to tear down walls, rebuild closets, replace windows and do wiring. And lo and behold, I could actually do it.

Of course when complications enter our family and personal stories, it is absolutely critical how we respond to them. Most people come into my office because of a complication that has entered their personal and family stories. My job is to ascertain what the complication is and help to put it right.

Devastating Complications

Death of a spouse. It's no accident that "death of a spouse" appears at the top of lists of stressful events. The pain of the loss can seem unyielding, unbearable. The sadness is intense. Anger—*How could you abandon me?*—and fear—*Whatever shall I do without you?*—stab at the widowed spouse. Thoughts of the lost spouse intrude even into sleep, invading one's dreams. The first year after the loss is the hardest, for each holiday, each celebration, each special event is faced for the first time without the lost loved one. There's the feeling that if I ever start crying, I'll never stop.

Grief is rarely a steady progression. The sufferer experiences it in fits and starts, moments of renewed happiness and joy followed by waves of sadness and loneliness. But as time marches by, for most the grieving process works healing, the pain lessens, and the widow gets on with life.

Some people, however, find themselves mired in grief. Sorrow lingers, often covering other more intense feelings of anger and guilt. Old business with the deceased has not been successfully completed.

Marge found herself stuck in grief. Her husband had died three years earlier. She had made his home office a monument to him. None of his possessions had been disturbed since his death. It was as if he would walk back into the house at any minute and resume his life there.

Marge spent long hours in her dead husband's office, staring at his picture, imagining his laugh, his walk, his touch. She was consumed by grief and unable to move on. Finally, at the urging of her children, she came to see me. She brought pictures and mementos of her lost husband. We talked of him and what he had meant to her. Then I began to probe the unfinished business that kept Marge entwined with him in grief.

Her husband had been unfaithful in the last several years before his death. He had strayed from Marge first emotionally, then physically. The two had been practically separated, with the husband spending most of his time with a girlfriend, when a sudden heart attack took him. Marge had felt responsible for his wanderings. She felt inadequate and guilty as a wife and lover. But she also was intensely angry with her husband for betraying her and never seeking the counseling she knew they desperately needed. All these feelings had been shoved out of her mind when he died, and she had come to idealize this man who had failed her so grievously.

Death of a parent. Losing a parent when one is a child is a traumatic event. Though the pain is severe for all children who experience this loss, the impact is lessened for a child who enjoys good relationships within the family before the death, receives timely and accurate information about the death, and has a caretaker who can give comfort and encourage the child to grieve.

Death of a child. Children are not supposed to precede parents in death. We are all supposed to live out a full life, marry, have children, and eventually die, leaving behind our spouse and children to mourn us. But death often takes people out of this sequence. Many bereaved parents find it impossible to completely forsake the grieving process even years later, sensing that to stop grieving would be an act of betrayal.

Sue Heiney, a nurse in an oncology treatment center, worked with a young girl who was dying of cancer. A bone-marrow transplant had not worked, and as the young girl lay dying her parents were distraught. On the night she died, Heiney says, she was restless and uncomfortable. To relieve her restlessness, her mother sat at her bedside and suggested that she imagine herself walking on a beach (Heiney had used this beach image during trying medical procedures to distract the girl from the pain).

Seeing that the girl had settled into the image of walking on the beach, the mother realized that she had to give her daughter permission to die. So she gently told her daughter that she could go on and "walk with Jesus if she wanted to." As the mother spoke these words, her daughter slipped into eternity.[3]

Suicide. Suicide is often a complication that haunts a family story for generations. David Treadway, a family counselor, tells how this particular complication unfolded in his own family. He grew up in the quaint village of Sturbridge, Massachusetts, where his parents owned an old inn. Years after his mother's death, he penned this letter to her:

Dear Mom,

I am writing at the old Sturbridge house, in Jon's bedroom. Soon, I'll be leaving for Williamstown and I'm trying to figure out what I want to say to you after all these years. Thinking about you still jams me up with feeling mad and sad and guilty.

I guess the time has come for me to forgive you for killing yourself. I've spent years romanticizing your death into a noble tragedy, with you as the forlorn heroine. Other times, I've been angry and blamed you for destroying the family with your singularly selfish choice. I've also felt so guilty because I avoided you like the plague for the last few years of your life, and I really didn't feel anything at all when you killed yourself.

I've never allowed myself to know how awful you must have felt. It's in the last self-portrait you painted. Your self-loathing is brutal to behold: the cold disdain in your eyes. Towards the end, I imagine that you lay in bed, filleting yourself with hatred, exaggerating every mistake or flaw, dismissing every accomplishment or talent and blaming yourself for everything that ever went wrong in our family. You must have felt a desperate craving for utter oblivion.

For years, I felt that I had forgiven you for murdering yourself. That was b—s—. Beneath the smoothly polished façade of forgiveness, I was dead inside. I hated you and I hated me for hating you. And I felt nothing at all.

It's been 26 years now. For most of that time, I never gave you a second thought. Now, I can't get you out of my mind. This is progress?

Mom, I think it's time to really forgive you, and maybe even me. But I'm still mad. I just don't know how to let go of it. Believe it or not, I've been trying to pray about it. I've also begun to write it all down. It's a form of prayer, too.

But I don't really know what I'm doing. I'm just here.

I've never said thank you, Mom. I've never really acknowledged how much love you gave all of us. How much the best part of me comes from the best part of you. I am proud to have been in your parade.

I'm blessed with a wonderful wife. You would like Kate. She doesn't buy any of my b—s—, and she loves me anyway. I also have two sons who fill my heart with joy and gratitude. (Not all the time, of course.) I wish you could meet them. I wish they could have met you. It's hard to explain suicide to them.

I finally did sail the Atlantic. I think you would have been proud of me. It's going to have to be enough though. I've decided not to cross the Pacific. I'm too old. I have learned to care enough to be afraid. I am the same age you were when you died.

There's really not much more to say. I'm sorry I've been so angry. I'm glad you were my Mom. You still are. I wish you were here.

Goodbye,

David[4]

Divorce. Divorce is wrenchingly painful to the people involved. I think I've talked to hundreds of people who have been divorced. For those who did not want the divorce, on whom the divorce was perpetrated, the sense of betrayal and rejection is overwhelming. In many ways the mourning following divorce parallels that of the death of a spouse, though anger eclipses other feelings in divorce.

Judith Wallerstein did a landmark study on the long-term effects of divorce on children.[5] She found that divorce becomes deeply woven into the personal story of the children who experience it, making them extremely reluctant to draw close to another in an intimate relationship when their turn to bond comes.

Abuse. Kerian Freeman is a survivor of one of the cruelest forms of betrayal, incest. At the age of thirty-seven he related his story in a journal article.[6] The secret of incest, he says, darkened every day of his life until he was thirty-three years old.

When Kerian was three years old, his mother died of cancer. Several months later his father began to use him sexually. At first his father would come to him late at night, when he assumed Kerian was asleep. But as time went by, his father would violate him in more perverse ways at any time during the evening. Like many men, this father confused emotional needs with sex. Now that his wife was gone, his neediness turned toward the most vulnerable family member, his three-year-old son.

At the age of fourteen Kerian began to experience the effects of the abuse, becoming suicidally depressed. He was terrified to ask a girl for a date. He found himself turned on sexually by men's bodies, yet didn't want to be gay. Then he began to fondle his six-year-old male cousin as he slept. Later he graduated to getting picked up by men for sexual experiences.

At the age of twenty-five, however, he married and moved to the suburbs. His relationship with his wife flourished, though his self-esteem was low. He met a counselor (he had been to others unsuccessfully) who helped him face the awful realities of his abuse. For the first time in his life, he says, he did not feel damaged or sick or neurotic.

Summing up his experience, Kerian Freeman writes:

Far from being harmless and unimportant, this incest had permeated my life, changed my perception of myself, my body, my sense of trust. Everything was degraded, cheapened, sickened— especially my sense of myself. My own body seemed to have betrayed me by attracting a kind of attention I didn't want from a man I needed and loved, and by getting aroused by, wanting, enjoying something that, at the same time, felt horrible and wrong.

My father, out of loneliness and need, had used me. Even though I had never been physically forced—indeed, almost because I hadn't been—I was as much a prisoner as any prisoner of war. Like a child in a battle zone, I handled my experience in the most effective way the human mind knows: I dissociated myself from what was happening to me. Night and day were two separate realities that I could not bring together. What happened had been so traumatic that I blocked it out of all daytime conscious memory. Now, almost 30 years later, I had to untangle the confusion once and for all and to learn to see and understand ways I still lived and thought like that victimized child.

Mental illness/substance abuse. Many children face the incapacitation of one or both parents. Sometimes a parent becomes mentally ill. At other times the incapacitation is self-inflicted in the form of substance abuse.

For many of these people, written into their stories are feelings of being isolated, uneasiness with people (especially authority figures) and fear of abandonment (which may tempt them to try almost anything to hold on to a relationship, or to draw away from commitment for fear of getting hurt). Unfortunately, because their family story included parents who were inconsistent in their availability and care, these people tend to choose insecure relationships (matching childhood experiences) and seek approval and affirmation from a person who just can't deliver. Intimacy becomes a threat. Getting close means getting hurt.

These folks also may feel "alone in a crowd" and "out of it" because of the lack of attachment experienced in their family of origin; they feel they are not like other people. They tend to feel very guilty when they stand up for themselves rather than giving in to others. So they live as victims, being reactors rather than actors. It is too frightening for them to take the initiative.

As children these people were "parentified." They never had a chance to be children; they were too busy taking care of their parents. As adults, they don't know how to play or what it feels like to have fun. They have an overdeveloped sense of responsibility and prefer to be concerned with others rather than themselves (or they may go to the other extreme and be totally irresponsible).

They can only guess what "normal" is. They have no frame of reference for what it is like to be in a normal household or what is OK to say and feel. As a result, they have difficulty trusting their own perceptions in situations. Their parents didn't validate reality, so as children they changed their internal reality to fit the chaos outside themselves.

Many of these people feel they must remain tightly in control for fear of getting out of control. Anger and other intense feelings are submerged through suppression, repression and denial. These folks need to manage the reactions of others because predicting reactions is futile. Their sense of self-worth is greatly enhanced when they feel they have matters under control.

They feel guilty when they want personal needs to be met. In childhood their needs were met only when their parents were able to attend to them, not when their internal reality dictated a need.

Murder. I once worked with a young boy who had watched his father shoot his mother, than kill himself. I have also worked with others who have experienced the murder of a close family member. This event has haunted them down through the years. Feelings of personal vulnerability emerge. *Why wasn't I the one?* they wonder.

Murder is brutal, senseless, meaningless. A life is taken, a story is completed long before it should have been. This complication jars the family story, sending it spiraling.

Others. Other serious complications involve loss of health, loss of financial position or loss of reputation. Each is devastating in its own way as it affects unfolding family and personal stories.

Understanding Complications

We would like to think that all complications, viewed after the passage of time, can be seen to have clear meaning in the unfolding story God is writing in our lives. But I have found that not all complications can be understood so clearly, even after many years pass.

After years of prayer and preparation, my brother and sister-in-law went to Peru as missionaries. They had overcome many obstacles to attain that goal, and we all expected that God would have them there for many years of ministry. After two years in Peru, they had a baby girl. Their first child had been a son, so they were ecstatic to add a daughter to the family. But then tragedy struck. The baby died unexpectedly one night after only two months of life.

My brother and his wife were devastated. They did not recover enough to be able to continue their ministry in Peru. They returned to the United States saddened and bewildered.

That was twenty-five years ago. Since then my brother has become a successful teacher and pastor, and my sister-in-law is a respected nurse. Yet the questions linger. Why was little Martha taken? What was the point of all that suffering?

More Modest Complications

Not all complications in a family story are so dramatic and life-changing. Each day seems filled with complications of a lesser sort.

Moving. In 1987 I did what had been unthinkable for me, my family and my friends. I decided to leave northern Virginia, where my family had lived for generations, and move to California to direct a counseling center in a church where my friend was the senior pastor. In twenty years of marriage, my wife and I had never lived outside Virginia. So it was for the first time in my life that I was experiencing the very disorienting complication of moving.

In California I had trouble finding my way home at night from my office. I couldn't find a thing in the supermarket. None of the landscapes seemed familiar. Inside I experienced an ongoing sense of disorientation. These feelings lasted to a greater or lesser degree for a year.

Moving presents us with physical relocation, the loss of familiar surroundings and disconnection from people we care about. But there's a deeper process that seems to unfold. As I sift through all my things, packing and unpacking, I reencounter memories. More energy is attached to certain items than to others. For example, for some picking up an old uniform rekindles memories of foxholes, bullets flying overhead, and fear.

Losing a job or acquiring a new job. People move from one job to another throughout life. For some the transition is not particularly unsettling. For others, especially those who are fired or otherwise terminated, the loss can be profound. When a person loses a job, she loses also the status, the daily routines, the affiliations with others, the income, the mental stimulation and certain choices.

After the loss comes the grief, a series of powerful feelings and questions:

1. Shock: *I lost it!*
2. Refusal to believe: *Not me!*
3. Anger: *Why me?*
4. Discouragement and depression: *Woe is me.*

5. Bargaining: *Why not this instead of me?*

6. Acceptance: *It's really me.*

Children, who rely on Mother and Father for security and stability, may find it most unsettling to see a parent devastated by job loss. The children's world is threatened, and stress tends to flow to the weakest link in the family system.

Loss of relationship. Friendships can slip away from us. Some friends seem to drift apart. Other friendships are torn apart by betrayal. But in each case, the loss of a friendship takes something important away from our life. I have lost several friendships over the years, and the thought of these lost friends still causes pain to me.

Celebrations and holidays. Even as I write this sentence, a party is unfolding downstairs from me. The wife of one of my partners just graduated from college, and all her family and friends have come to celebrate with her. *Doesn't seem much like a complication,* you might think. But these celebrations that punctuate our lives do have an element of complication to them. We come to them with expectations of pleasure, and we may be sadly disappointed in the actual experience.

Transitions and separations. Life is filled with comings and goings. Problems often develop in families when someone is either coming (birth of a child, mother-in-law moves in) or going (children go off to college, spouse dies). Letting go of family members can be extremely difficult in certain family stories, especially those in which the characters are deeply emotionally involved with each other. Children may become too important to parents, having been drawn into conflicts raging between the mother and father. Single parents often pull children into their emotional lives inappropriately, seeking support and nurture from them. Such children may find separation from the family very painful, because they have become too important to the life and health of parents.

On the other extreme, some parents are extremely neglectful of their children, essentially leaving the young ones to raise themselves. These children tend to feel too separated from parents and long for more nurture and care. These children often feel ill-defined and grope for identity without the guiding hand of a loving parent.

Interruptions. Interruptions in our daily routines confront each of us. This is one reason that being a homemaker is so difficult. A homemaker is constantly interrupted. Some days it seems that just as we are getting into a routine, hitting our creative edge, getting "into the groove," someone comes in, or phones, and interrupts the flow we've established.

Life is filled with interruptions. It's helpful, though, to read through the Gospels and note how much of Jesus' ministry came about through interruptions. He seemed to thrive on them. He'd be walking somewhere to teach, and all at once someone would be hanging on him, hoping to gain a favor, settle a dispute or receive a healing touch. Arguably Jesus' ministry was *in* the interruptions, not in spite of them.

Are Complications Defining Moments?

We are able to survive the most devastating of complications if we have two components firmly in place: we know who we are *(I am defined),* and we know what we are here for *(I have a purpose).* What makes these two personality components possible is the character of God. When we cannot clearly see God in the midst of complications, when we cannot feel his hand at work in our lives as the suffering mounts, we rely on his character, knowing who he is. Knowing who God is, then who I am, then what I am here for changes my whole perspective on life.

The danger of the great complications that arise in our lives is that they can define us in negative ways *(I'm nothing but a rape victim).* As I become defined in a certain way, my character changes, my purpose is altered, and my story shoots off in a different direction.

I have always been haunted by Psalm 73. When I first read it, I was startled that it was in the Bible. But now that I have talked with thousands of people about the complications that have flooded their lives, this poem makes complete sense. The psalmist begins with an appropriate proposition: "God is good . . . to those who are pure in heart" (v. 1). Everyone agrees with this. But beginning in verse 2, things begin to come apart as the psalmist runs headlong into a complication. For some reason he loses his footing. As this happens, the first casualty is his objectivity: "The wicked have no problems, they're always carefree" (see vv. 3-12). In the midst of the psalmist's suffering, he slips into despair (vv. 13-16). Finally, though, he is able (and I've wondered how long it took him to get to this place—perhaps it was years) to gain perspective and see that the wicked are in a vulnerable position and that the only tenable place to stand is in God's presence.

As the plot of your family story has unfolded, you may have found yourself asking, *What does this all mean anyway? Why did this child die? Why did I lose my job? What was the point of my child running away from home?* Perhaps the answers to these questions have already come. But they may not have come. An incident remains lodged in the back of your mind, a story fragment that has not been adequately resolved. You will be strengthened as you place your trust in God's *character,* even though you cannot see his hand clearly in this situation yet.

Plot Lines over the Generations

Family plots have a way of recurring down through the generations. The same themes, the same conflicts, even the very same stories and dialogues seem to repeat from one generation to the next. That is why some psychologists who do family therapy work almost exclusively with the past, having clients discern how the themes of their family story have recurred in cycles.

In Sally's family, the major plot involved women being used and discarded by unscrupulous men. Sally's grandmother and mother, and now she herself, had been used sexually as young women by much older married men who promptly discarded them. Indeed, Sally had been conceived in this way. She had never known her real father. At the age of twenty-three, she was now involved with a married man in his forties who obviously was merely using her for his own needs.

One of the most dangerous recurring plot lines involves the age and circumstances at which people die in a family story. Countless people have told me something like this: "All the men in my family die of cancer around age forty-four. I just hope I can get beyond this." This plot complication can become an expectation for the males in that family.

Exercise. Set up a chart like the one below and list the most prominent complications that have occurred in your life (child dying, moving, loss of job, friends leaving). List the date and complication. Then remember your decision process—how you went about deciding what you needed to do to get out of or through the complication. Next write the outcome—how the complication changed you and your personal and/or family story. See if you can note God's hand in each complication.

Year(s)	Complication	Decision process	Outcome

If you wish, you can flesh out your story by examining these important complications more closely. In your journal, write answers to the following questions about each: Who was significant in your life just before the complication occurred? What were their roles in the complication (antagonist, encourager or other)? What were your emotions before, during and after the complication?

Discovering Your Unique Family Plot

The plot in your family is a direct outworking of the premise. Once you have established the premise of your family (acceptance, competence or control), you can begin to see how the plot was built on this premise.

Certain plot lines logically flow from each of the premises. From *acceptance* come plot lines such as the following:

☐ Love: "He gave up everything for her. Their love was so beautiful."

☐ Rescue: "We saved the wastrel from disaster."

☐ Sacrifice: "She gave her all for her family. And they just kicked her in the teeth."

Some *competence* plot lines include the following:

☐ Underdog: "We never had much, but we always managed to land on top."

☐ Achievement: "It was a pure rags-to-riches story."

☐ Winning: "He'll do anything to get ahead."

Control may produce the following:

☐ Rivalry: "I was so much better than he was."

☐ Revenge: "I'll get even with you."

☐ Victim: "I am always overpowered by people who are stronger, more intelligent, more resourceful, luckier."

Some of the same plot themes can develop differently under different premises. Take the plot line of achievement. As a competence plot line, the story unfolds with the hero achieving great things to prove how competent he is. As a control plot line, achievements are acquired to stay on top, to master situations, to control others.

The premise sets the overall theme. Then the particular characters, interacting in the particular setting, unfold the plot as they are presented with various complications. Different families can be presented the same complications and end up with radically different plot lines. That's because each family brings a different set of ingredients to the complication.

Even the family dialogue is shaped by the premise and unfolding plot, as the family filters experiences through the lens of premise, making assumptions and speaking interpretations accordingly. "Look at his grades—all A's," Mother says proudly (stating a fact that is clearly printed on the report card). "That'll show the Joneses that we're better than they are," Father says (interpreting the report card from a control premise). Another father might say, "That's what we expect from anyone who bears the Smith name. Don't let me ever see anything but A's" (interpreting the report card from a competence premise).

The complication of extreme financial deprivation can lead to a number of plot lines, depending on the premise in a particular family. In competence families the plot often develops into a "rags-to-riches" scenario, where characters born in deprivation are able to elevate themselves to great achievement in various realms.

Exercise. Think of one or two plot lines (helpful or harmful) that existed in your family, and write a paragraph or two about each delineating how the plot played out over time in your family. Try to include all the characters in the family, even if some of them seemed to play no role in this plot line.

For example: "*Drunk night.* Dad would come home drunk on Friday night. Mom would get angry at him and start to hit him. I would rush in between them to try to separate them. My sister would sit in her room and shake."

Myths

Over generations, family members often fashion myths about the family story. A myth involves an explanation, though not really true, of what the story is all about. A myth is a ritualized premise. "Your grandparents struggled to make ends meet through the Depression, battling all odds, holding off the creditors, while building a grocery store that became the envy of the county." At the base of the myth is a kernel of truth that is embellished. But myths have a way of ignoring ambiguities and slanting stories in particular directions to prove points.

The unfolding myth sets the overall tone of the family story. Listen to the way people relate their family stories. Some will relate the story as a tragedy. "My mother and father had to struggle all their lives. They never had two nickels to rub together. They never had any breaks in life." Others will relate the story as a comedy. "Dad would always crack me up. No matter what the situation, he always had a joke. Never seemed to take anything too seriously." Still others will relate the story as a mystery. "Mom never knew why her parents had given her up for adoption. In fact, there were so many unanswered questions in her background." Others will relate the story as an adventure, or primarily a romance, or even a tale of horror. "There were so many things at the farm we couldn't explain. Animals would turn up sick and die, for no apparent reason. Mom seemed out of her mind most of the time."

A myth can point to deeper truths of the family story. It can also distort facts beyond all recognition and deny painful memories, driving family members into silence. The particular facts of the family stories are interpreted according to the family premise and how each character in the family perceives him- or herself. This is the stuff of myth.

Sometimes a family myth is the exact opposite of what has really been happening in the family. The denial of the true story line is so strong, possibly over many generations, that to recognize it would require family members to expend monumental energy. Often I see these families come into counseling because one or more family members have become very disturbed, perhaps falling into rage or depression. Their symptoms point to the disparity between the family myth and the reality.

Many families, for example, cherish the myth that all is peace and light. "We never disagree. We're all in perfect harmony." Usually lurking under the surface of these families is considerable disagreement and resentment that is never given an avenue to be aired and resolved, precisely because the family myth stands in the way.

One woman told me that in her family no one could ever speak a dissenting word, much less a harsh word about anyone or anything. Disagreements were immediately squelched: "We're just a perfectly wonderful, gracious family where all is sweetness and light." Her brother was now in jail for a variety of infractions, but no one discussed this. A sister had had a baby out of wedlock, but this again was not a subject to be discussed.

She herself was now married and had a family. Her husband

complained that when the two of them disagreed (his family had been very open and confrontational), she would always withdraw and refuse to discuss the issue. Needless to say, issues had mounted up between them. But for her the myth was "Peace and Harmony," and anything that contradicted this was ignored.

Other families harbor alcoholism for years, even for generations, because of family myths that absolutely do not allow for a family member who is a drunk. The devastating consequences on future generations have been detailed by Adult Children of Alcoholics. In fact, all the behaviors that tend now (rightly or wrongly) to be labeled as addictions (sex, gambling and the like) begin in families where that particular behavior is denied and covered up with a more satisfying family myth. Here the myth and family secrets join hands in a menacing way (this will be discussed further in chapter seven).

Exercise. Journal or discuss the following.

1. Have there been any discernible myths in your family? How have those myths affected the overall functioning of the family?

2. Have these myths served to cover family problems that should have been brought to the surface and resolved? If so, write about the problems and how you think these should have been handled in the past.

Endings

Someone once said that everyone's story is a tragedy, because every hero finally dies. But for the Christian this of course is not the case, because death does not end the story. We are part of a much larger Story that has been unfolding since the dawn of time and will continue to unfold until the end of time. Our family stories also continue through us to our children and beyond through the generations.

But it is true for all of us that certain personal stories end better than others, or at least appear to.

Exercise

1. Think about the premise in your family, the plot line(s) that developed from that premise and the myths that accompanied them.

Write these in your journal or discuss them with a close friend.

2. Prayerfully notice which elements of the unfolding story have been destructive. (For example, "My family story was a tragedy. Therefore I see myself as a helpless victim of circumstances who has no choices.") With the help of a friend or an accountability group, begin to formulate a strategy for changing the story.

Mike, for example, comes from a family story in which everyone is a victim. An accountability group helps him see that in most situations he tends not to initiate action but goes along with the crowd, then complains when nothing turns out the way he'd hoped. The group helps him formulate the following strategy: For three weeks he is to initiate one action with his wife (perhaps asking her out to dinner, or just asking her to walk around the block). He is then to record the results of his initiatives.

The group also notices that even in Mike's prayers he waits on God to do things and never springs into action ("Oh God, make me a better person—more patient and loving and helpful to others"). The group helps Mike put together a personal mission statement that includes specific character qualities he wants to develop, followed by strategies for achieving each. Following is a chart that summarizes Mike's plan.

Character quality	Strategy to achieve it	Results obtained
Community service (service)	Volunteer at a nursing home once a month	Currently a regular volunteer at home
More loving to wife (love)	Do one small personal thing for her daily	Currently has list of personal things wife likes; does one daily
Intentionally involved with children (patience)	Select one activity per child per week to do	Currently does this each week

7
The Story's Dialogue

Y*ou hateful, thoughtless* brute." Mary fumed at Bill as the session in my office marched toward a climax.

"I'm a brute?" Bill feigned bewilderment. "Me?" Bill's animation was something new. To this point, he had always been withdrawn and soft-spoken. "It is you who does the intimidation. You who overpower me to the point that I never feel as though I can collect my thoughts. And it's not just me, it's everybody."

"I don't suppose I should say anything." Marie began to speak, which surprised not only me but the other Simmons family members as well. "I don't usually say much in the family. But I do think it's important that we not be too critical of each other. Mom and Dad, I can't stand this fighting. It's not good for me. It's not good for Billy. He's been through a lot, and I think he's learned his lesson."

"Learned his lesson?" Julie began to lose the poised demeanor she fought so strenuously to maintain. "He's put Mom and Dad through hell the last several years, now gone to jail, and you think he's learned his lesson. What makes you think so?"

Bill and Mary had now broken off their confrontation of each other. Marie's interjection had effectively deflected their discussion. I wondered if Marie often served to deflect family conflict.

"Now girls," Mary began, wanting to ease the tension between her daughters.

"I'm wondering"—I jumped in—"if conflict in this family is too scary for everyone. Mom and Dad were fighting, and Marie, you stepped in to defuse that. Then you and Julie began to disagree, and Mom stepped into defuse *your* disagreement."

"It is scary in this family!" Now Billy broke into the discussion. "No one ever fights, or should ever fight, because we're supposed to be such a good example to the community."

"Does that mean that no one ever disagrees and nothing ever gets resolved?" I asked. For a moment the whole family sat in silence, reflecting on my question.

Bill finally spoke. "I'm afraid that may be true. And I don't know that it's been good for anybody."

"So most of your family discussions, at least when these came to disagreements, have been under the surface," I stated.

"Yes, that's true," Mary affirmed.

"Seems to me, then, that there must be a whole lot of issues in the family that have never been resolved, because they were too hot to handle. They've just been pushed under the rug, where they've caused problems," I continued.

"Afraid so." Bill looked down at his feet again.

"Well, this might be the place to start," I said. "What if we talk about how we can make it safe enough in this family for conflict and disagreements to occur? Then people can air their differences, be heard and feel safe, and get resolution." Now I felt as though we had a direction for this family, a way toward healing. If the disagreements that had plagued this family could be aired and resolved, family members would be able to get on with their lives and not feel stuck in old, unresolved battles.

The Importance of Dialogue

Dialogue, or communication, is critical to the unfolding story. Words are powerful instruments wielded by characters in the story. For words not only reveal who we are inside but also go out from us to do our bidding. Yet words are only part of dialogue. Meaning is communicated between people in many different ways, most of which are nonverbal.

Dialogue in the family story functions in a number of ways:

☐ It delineates character. It differentiates characters and makes them individual. In dialogue individual character is revealed. The ancient Hebrews understood that words, as they are spoken, reveal the essence of a speaker.

☐ It reveals the speaker. As I speak, the essence of who I am (self) comes out to you in verbal and nonverbal form. My words, backed up by my nonverbal communications, represent my self. Communication and deeds, then, are not qualitatively different. What I say and what I do are integral parts of my communication.

☐ It conveys information. We know things because someone has communicated with us.

☐ It relays emotion. Seventy percent of all communication is nonverbal. Through my posture, tone of voice, rate of speech and facial expressions, I can communicate a whole range of emotions.

☐ It sets boundaries between characters. Actually boundaries between people are set in a number of ways, dialogue being one of those ways.

☐ It sets the tone of the action in the family story.

Arguably dialogue is the greatest single factor affecting a person's health and relationship to others. For it is in the act of dialoguing that people connect with one another, for good or for ill.

How I Say What I Say

Messages arise from and are perceived in different areas within our brain. That's because our brain contains two brains in one: the emotional brain and the logical brain, the "heart" and "head." As a result, we are capable of knowing in two different ways. Paul's words in Romans 10:9 seem to take account of this: "confess with your mouth [the logical brain uses words] . . . and believe in your heart."

My emotional brain initially asks the question *Am I safe? Are you friend or foe?* Then it monitors and expresses emotion: if you're friend I'm happy; if you're foe I'm frightened. Emotions act as guides as we negotiate situations that intellect alone cannot address (danger, loss, perseverance, intimacy, family story writing). All emotions are impulses to act (anger, for example, is an impulse to attack; fear is an impulse to flee).[1]

Then, ideally acting in harmony with the emotional brain, there's the logical brain, divided into two parts:

☐ The left brain, where words are produced and processed, where logical concepts are strung together and understood, where explanations of the world are manufactured and dispensed. This side breaks things down into component parts to see the detail.

☐ The right brain, where relationship is monitored.

Because the brain has these different areas that attend to the world slightly differently (though in concert with the other parts of the brain), communication is multidimensional. There are no straightforward messages. Let's look at a diagram to see how messages are sent and received between two people.

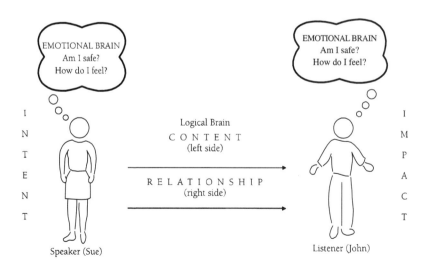

Figure 4. Message sending and receiving

The speaker (Sue) begins with a particular intent *(I want John to get up and close the door)*. She goes to her left brain and fashions a sentence using proper English words, grammar and syntax. She then speaks the message to John: "John, close the door."

John's emotional brain first scans the situation to determine whether he is safe. If it is determined that he is not safe, he will either run or fight. No other parts of Sue's communication are processed until the safety issue is determined. John does determine that he is safe, so he picks up the content of the message (the words put together in Sue's sentence) on the left side of his brain. Simultaneously, the right side of his brain scans Sue to determine the relationship message *(what is the relationship like between us?)*.

We know a lot about the content of messages. We spend most of our formal schooling figuring out these messages, how to form them and how to understand them. But we are given precious little instruction in understanding relationship messages.

Relationship messages are formed not by words but by our bodies as we speak. A message such as "Close the door!" can be said in many different ways. It is the *way* a content message is said that determines the relationship message. Because the right brain works out of the spotlight, while the left brain takes center stage, its work is usually unnoticed. This makes relationship messages even more powerful. We don't sit down and think about how we want these messages to be; they just emerge automatically.

We send relationship messages outside of awareness. We also receive these messages outside of awareness. So critical relationship messages are constantly being passed back and forth between us, and we don't consciously know it. But the fact that we aren't consciously aware of these messages doesn't mean that we don't act on them. We act on them all the time, reacting to insignificant comments as though the world were ending, blowing up when someone makes a simple request, steering clear of certain people because we just don't feel right around them.

Relationships are formed and brokered quite beyond our awareness, especially if we tend to be more "left-brained," logic-oriented people. Obviously, certain people are much more in tune with relationship messages and learn to read and understand them thoroughly. But the majority of people go through life unaware of the impact these messages are having on them.

Components of Relationship Messages

The very first relationship-message sender is the eye. As we talk with each other, our eyes are communicating volumes about the relationship. Pupils dilate and constrict. The eye darts back and forth, up and down, or stays focused. Eye contact is made or not made with the listener. Following are examples of the relationship messages sent by the eyes.

Behavior	Relationship message
I don't look at the listener.	You're unimportant to me.
	I'm ashamed of myself.
My eyes dart as I speak.	I'm anxious about our relationship.
My pupils are dilated.	I'm open to you and feel safe.
My pupils are constricted.	I'm closed to you and don't feel safe.

Next in importance are posture and movement. As we talk, we scan the listener to see how he or she is responding to our messages. In turn, the listener scans us to read the critical relationship messages that are sent through the way we stand and walk.

One experimenter watched people conversing with each other and saw that various postural changes occurred as they spoke. He found that when two people are in agreement on the subject they are discussing, they assume a similar posture. As their attitudes on the discussed subject continue in agreement, they begin to move almost in mirror image to each other.[2] Slow-motion filming of this phenomenon has shown that there is a "microsynchrony" of small movements, hard to see with the naked eye. These movements include tiny, momentary dips and nods of the head, tensing of fingers, stretching of lips and jerks of the body that become matched when two people have strong rapport. Evidently the right side of the brain unconsciously registers the movements of the other and matches these through similar movements; the other person's right brain registers a feeling of warmth in response.

Desmond Morris called these small, incidental motions "nonverbal leakage," important actions that give us away, revealing our true feelings and intentions without our knowledge.[3] Our emotional brain has a way of exposing us, even when we try to hide our true selves.

The Bible has a lot to say about how our emotional brain gives away our true convictions. James seems to have had this in mind when he said, "Faith without works is dead" (see Jas 2:14-26). Words of faith that are not backed up by the incidental actions of the speaker is null and void. "Why do you call me, 'Lord, Lord,' and do not do what I say?" Jesus said (Lk 6:46).

Next in importance in relationship messages are gestures and facial expressions. A gesture is any action that sends a visual signal to an onlooker. We are so accustomed to the gestures taking place constantly around us that we tend not to take particular notice of them. They seem to be present merely as a punctuation to our existence.

Morris discusses two types of gestures. *Incidental* gestures such as cleaning, rubbing, wiping, coughing, yawning and stretching carry secondary messages to the listener. Often just by observing these incidental gestures you can correctly guess a person's mood and how she feels about her relationship with you.

Primary gestures, by contrast, involve deliberate signaling. The hands and face are the most important primary gesturers. The human face, made up of countless muscles, is capable of myriad poses. In fact, the face transmits the bulk of nonverbal signaling. The subtle changes that our faces make as we talk with someone constantly send information to that person about the relationship. The eyebrow position alone can convey moods of dismay, anger and joy.[4]

Next are voice and vocal variety. People constantly adjust tone, tempo and amplitude as they speak. When these changes are dramatic, we notice them consciously. If the changes are more subtle, we receive them unconsciously on the right side of our brain. My voice can sound harsh, conveying to the listener that I feel powerful and blaming. My voice can be soft and conciliatory. My voice can waver, signaling doubt and uncertainty.

Congruent and Incongruent Messages

Our dialogue is congruent when what we say (left brain) and the nonverbal messages we send (right brain) match each other. Often, unfortunately, our dialogue becomes incongruent and our words fail to match our nonverbal communications. We are particularly vulnerable to incongruity when we become anxious. At these moments our dialogue tends to disassemble: our nonverbal messages mask what we actually experience inside, even though our words may speak to the contrary. At such times we may assume any of four different postures:

☐ *Placate*—a cringing, pleading, whining, one-down posture. This person tries to please everyone so as to avoid any hint of disagreement and conflict. He or she fears that the other person will become angry and rejecting.

☐ *Blame*—a shouting, accusing, finger-wagging, one-up posture. This person, acting as the boss, points an accusing finger at others, thus fomenting a great deal of conflict. Underneath the bluster is usually a frightened individual who fears being blamed for a situation that felt out of his or her control.

☐ *Computer*—a rigid, expressionless, monotone posture. This person is ultra-reasonable, with not the slightest hint of emotion. Conflict for him is always addressed with a series of propositional statements. The computerlike approach usually masks vulnerability.

☐ *Distract*—an irrelevant, faltering, misdirected posture. This person never sticks to the subject at hand. As conflict builds, he or she distracts all combatants into other issues.

These postures grow out of the character we have come to be and the roles that we assume in the family story. If my character in the family involves being spineless and self-deprecating, and my role is peacemaker, I will undoubtedly assume a placating posture when I become anxious (which is when characters in the family story begin to stir into disagreement, and conflict looms).

We will not necessarily assume the same roles and postures in other story settings. Many people go off to work and assume a whole new role. Sometimes whole families assume the same incongruent postures. Remember, people are multidimensional and can display many different parts of themselves, given the dictates of the particular story in which they find themselves. As we assume a different role, we also take on different postures in our communication.

Irony

In storytelling, irony is the discrepancy between reality and what is said or perceived to be true. It is a major source of comedy in fiction. Irony permeates our unfolding family stories also: the mother finally gets around to meticulously washing the kitchen floor, and no sooner has she put the mop away than the baby spills orange juice right in the middle of her finished work.

One of the ironic twists that I discover over and over in families with difficulties involves attempts at solutions to family problems. This phenomenon is called "The Solution Becomes the Problem." Here's how it works. A problem develops in a family—say daughter Jenny develops an eating problem, eating junk food to excess, and becomes overweight. Father sees this problem developing in his daughter, so he comes up with a solution (*I will continually point out this problem to Jenny, so she will be aware of her overeating and stop*). The wrong solution is developed because the nature of the problem is misunderstood (Jenny overeats because she is anxious, not because she is careless).

Unfortunately, once a solution is generated we usually have difficulty changing our way of looking at the problem. So our feeble attempts at solutions become problem generators themselves. The more Father reminds Jenny that she is overeating and becoming fat, the more she eats. And the more she eats, the more Father points out to her the overeating. Our only response when our solution doesn't seem to work is to apply *more* of the same solution.

This procedure would be funny if it weren't for the dire consequences that obviously ensue. Yet the way a solution becomes the problem can be seen over and over again in family dialogue:

☐ "My teenage son won't listen when I lecture him. I'll lecture him more."

☐ "My wife drinks too much. I'll badger her about it constantly until she quits."

☐ "My husband constantly tries to make conversation with me when I'm reading. I'll ignore him until he goes away."

I think it's Alcoholics Anonymous that teaches its members, "Mental illness is doing the same thing over and over again, expecting different results."

Ted Williams, the Boston Red Sox star of a generation ago, had the best solution. He said, "When you're in a slump (in his case, batting slump), change your stance." Changing our stance vis-à-vis a problem requires us to stop, take note of the nature of the problem and our misperceptions of it, and then generate a new solution. Often we don't take the time, so we merely allow ourselves to fall back into the very patterns that continue to generate the old problem.

Patterns of Communication in the Family Story

Not only our communication but also the *patterns* of our communication are important. Patterns involve whom we talk to, when and how we talk, covering which subjects, and many other elements.

Communication flows through a family without much notice. A mother talks lovingly to one child, with disdain to another, ignoring a third. A father is shuffled to the sidelines of family life because what he has to say is deemed irrelevant. Certain topics are carefully avoided. Others are discussed in great detail.

I once worked with a family whose children had all grown to adulthood. The mother had died, leaving the father alone. I had the whole family come in—brothers and sisters with their father. The mother had been the family "phone operator," the hub of the wheel. All communication was channeled through her. If a brother wanted to know something about his sister, he didn't ask the sister; he asked Mother, who told him.

Obviously, when Mother died communication became a problem within the family. Siblings found that they had very little relationship with each other. Everything had been brokered through Mother. The oldest son finally said to his sister, "Look, sis, I know you'd like to have a closer family. But I really don't know you. I wouldn't know where to begin." Unfortunately this family departed from my office and remained isolated from each other.

In another family I worked with, the father's role was to calm the waters and smooth over all rough spots so that there was never any conflict. Whenever conflict brewed, he would immediately insert himself between the combatants, explaining each to the other and blocking any disagreements. When I finally got him to stop this ("It's not your responsibility, plus the children never learn how to manage conflict for themselves"), there was a great deal of tension in the family: each member, beginning with his wife, attempted to get him back into his role. Finally everyone realized that Dad would not change back to his old role, and the other family members learned to deal with each other more effectively.

Exercise. Take a moment to think of your family dialogue patterns.

1. What pairs of people in the family do the most dialoguing (for example, mother-daughter, sister-sister)? Can you perceive any particular patterns in this? (For example: "The females do 90 percent of the talking. Dad never seems to talk with anyone.")

2. What topics are the most discussed—politics, sports, fashions? Which topics are avoided—for example, sex, Dad's drinking?

Secrets and Silences

In the fall of 1994, Susan Smith, a young divorced mother of two small boys, strapped her children in the back of her car, drove to a nearby lake, put the gear in neutral and watched as the car slipped into the lake, taking her children to their deaths. As Smith stood trial for murder the next year, secrets began to emerge about her life and the life of the small South Carolina town (population ten thousand) in which she had been born and raised.

Friends of Smith were astonished by the secrets she had hidden from everyone over the years. Her final year in school, the year she was voted friendliest in her class, she swallowed a handful of Anacin in an aborted attempt to kill herself. It was not her first or last attempt. Her father had committed suicide when she was six. At fifteen her stepfather had begun to molest her sexually. Her mother knew it and did nothing. By sixteen she was having affairs with the forty-year-old manager and the thirty-year-old assistant manager at the grocery where she worked.

After high-school graduation she took a job at a company where she was the cheerful life of the party, making sure everyone was included in company functions. No one knew she was sleeping with both the millionaire boss and his son.

Touch a town, touch a nation, or touch a family deeply, and you will find a secret. Secrets usually hide truths associated with guilt and shame.[5] We have habits and addictions (alcohol, sex, drugs) that we dare not share. Horrible things (being molested, beaten, ridiculed) have happened to us and enveloped us. We have done things to others that we fear will be revealed. Our thoughts at times run wild, painting weird, kinky pictures we know would destroy our reputation.

In a family, silence often grows up around topics too painful to be discussed. These issues lie right out in the open, everyone knows about them, but no one is supposed to speak of them.

Secrets are a little different from silences. Secrets are parts of the story that are kept hidden from certain members of the family. Frank Pittman, a family psychiatrist, says that secrets involve information that is kept from people who need it.[6] Understood this way, secrets are dangerous realities, not just minor unpleasantries. They have a nasty way of altering who we are.

Why do we keep secrets in our family stories? We keep them to protect ourselves and those we love from pain. Those things we keep secret are the things that we are ashamed of. To remember them causes a great deal of pain to the secret-keeper. Yet we believe that exposing the secret would bring undue pain to the one who heard the secret.

We also keep secrets because we are afraid. We fear what will happen if the truth were known. *I know Johnny would leave me if he knew that I had a child out of wedlock and gave it up for adoption.*

Unfortunately, secrets have a way of wrapping a family in shame. Shame then becomes a powerful motivator for certain people, driving them toward perfection and control. It can also drive us toward addictive behaviors in an attempt to mask the pain. But what makes secrets so harmful is the fact that when an issue is kept secret *it cannot be dealt with*. It just lies there, under the surface, unexamined and festering, spreading its poison throughout the family story.

Secrets are often kept through generations as older generations refuse to speak and the young are intimidated into silence. I've seen families in which the daughter, mother, grandmother and great-grandmother all had children out of wedlock. Sex was never discussed by any of them; it was a taboo subject altogether (as of course were the out-of-wedlock pregnancies). But each mother in turn had been extremely anxious about the sexual development of each daughter, hoping that she would not repeat the same dreadful error. Unfortunately, each daughter followed the mother with a pregnancy.

Secrets have a way of forming and maintaining coalitions between family members. Family members can be allied with certain members and alienated from others by secrets. One mother, who tried to swear me to secrecy, told me that her husband was an alcoholic. I then talked with several of the children. When I broached the subject of their father's drinking, each of the children became fearful and did not want to continue the discussion. The oldest daughter had entered into a coalition with the mother to aid her in her distress. Several of the younger children were allied with the father's mother to keep peace in the family. The family terminated counseling prematurely, unable to face the ugly secrets that plagued them.

Health	Family history
Epilepsy	Faked or denied ethnicity/race
Mental illness	Traumas
Venereal disease	Holocaust survivors
AIDS	Physical or sexual abuse
Chronic illness	
	Self-destruction
Finances	Addictions
Theft	Anorexia nervosa/bulimia
Embezzlement	Suicide attempts
Poverty	Mutilation
Bankruptcy	
Income loss	**Abuse**
	Beatings
Relationships	Rape
Extramarital affairs	Incest
Adoption dishonest	
Death	**Sexual**
	Gay or lesbian relationships
	Sexual identity
	Abortions
	Births for adoption

Table 5. Source events for secrets[7]

Secrets are very powerful influences in the development of the individual ("if you knew I had an abortion, you would never have married me") and family stories ("in our family we never mention the fact that Junior has AIDS"). Examples of events that may lead to secrets are listed in table 5.

Philip was never told he was adopted. His parents lied about the time of year they were married and the circumstances surrounding Philip's birth. As he grew, he asked questions about his physical features (because they resembled neither parent), his parents' wedding pictures (which seemed to reveal a different season of the year from the time he had been told) and other aspects of their marriage and his birth. With each question his parents became apprehensive and told a lie. Philip was confused about his perceptions (which were accurate, but denied by his parents).

A great deal of energy is expended in maintaining secrets. Issues are avoided. Lies are concocted. People become extremely intense when certain topics are introduced in conversation or even while watching TV. The following sequence shows how secrets tend to develop in families:

☐ I do something shameful, or something shameful is done to me. I am extremely intense about it.

☐ I keep this issue a secret (from my spouse, my children, my parents).

☐ I cannot effectively deal with this issue myself (or seek help to handle it), nor can I allow family members to assist me in handling it *(we will not discuss this—it is a secret).*

☐ Because the issue has not received attention that would lead to healing and forgiveness, I am wounded here; later I am unable to assist my children in discussing this issue and dealing with it effectively in their own lives.

☐ As my children move toward this area, I'm fearful; I overreact but remain unable to discuss the issue effectively. I insist that the issue not be discussed. Lack of clarity about the issue, along with the intensity that surrounds it, actually attracts family members toward the issue, making it more—not less—likely that they will experience the same thing I did.

Disclosing and discussing family secrets is remarkably freeing. Folks are usually amazed that the sky doesn't fall when finally the family can openly discuss Mother's drinking, Brother's arrest, Dad's gambling, Sister's promiscuity. Nevertheless, I don't recommend that every secret be blurted out at the next family gathering. People have to take into account their particular situations.

Exercise. Think back on your family as you were growing up. List one or two secrets that you now know were held in the family. Note why you think these were kept secret, and the impact of these secrets on the unfolding family story.

Now list several issues the family has kept silent about (for example, "Father dropped his muddy shoes in the middle of the living room, but no one, not even Mom, said a thing"). Why do you suppose these issues were never allowed to be discussed? What was the impact of not discussing them?

Family Coalitions

Coalitions form where family members join together in various group-
ings, often at the expense of other members. Coalitions aren't necessarily bad. Parents need a coalition to run the family effectively.

Coalitions become sinister when two family members of different
generations join against a third member. For example, a grandmother
joins with her granddaughter against the younger girl's mother (the
grandmother's daughter). Or a father joins with his son to defeat his
wife in certain ways.

In these situations the power of the adult in the coalition is heightened. The child is also given too much power. And the power of the
adult against whom the coalition is aimed is greatly diminished.[8] This
unbalances the family, and the coalitions solidify into polarizations.
Family members then leave their preferred roles and take on roles that
oppose other members. Parents find themselves enemies of each other.
Brothers and sisters become rivals.

Becky is eleven years old. Her mother and father do not get along.
Becky's father is in a coalition with her against her mother. Whenever
Mom attempts to set appropriate boundaries of behavior with Becky,
Dad jumps in, reprimands Mom and dismantles any boundaries Mom
has put in place. Mom and Dad fight constantly. Becky's younger
brother is extremely jealous of her favored position with Dad.

Jeff is sixteen. His mother is divorced. She pulls him into a coalition
with her against her father, who has come to live with the family and
help his daughter out in childrearing. Whenever Jeff's grandfather
attempts to set limits with him, Jeff laughs at him, and Jeff's mom tells
her father to "back off."

Bernice is forty-two and married to Mark. Bernice has formed a
coalition with Mark's mother against him. The two women often talk
on the phone about Mark's latest transgressions. When Mark invites
his parents over for supper, invariably he finds himself entangled in
squabbles, with his wife allied with his mother against him. His father
chooses to stay out of the fray.

Usually coalitions across generational lines are denied by the people involved. But the destructive power of these arrangements is obvious. Husband and wife, the normal authorities within the family, are compromised, so that the adults find themselves unable to adequately set the direction of the family. Certain family members are given extra responsibility, influence and resources. Other family members are given less. The family becomes paralyzed, tensions mount, and symptoms often develop in one or more family members.

Leveling

Leveling is the ideal practice in dialogue, for when we level our dialogue is accurate. To be accurate, dialogue needs several crucial elements.

1. *I must speak what is true.* In some ways each word that I speak to you is a promise, a promise of authenticity: "My words coming out to you now are true and accurate. I promise."

2. *I must be congruent.* What I say matches the way I feel. My tone of voice, posture and facial expressions (body language) match the way that I truly feel.

3. *I must speak the whole truth.* Leveling within a family story requires the absence of crippling secrets. Issues are clearly understood and discussed.

4. *I must speak the whole truth to the right people.* Destructive, cross-generational coalitions are avoided. Parents are free to join together as the family's authority figures to bring about order and set the direction of the unfolding story.

Exercise

1. Take a moment to think of how communication flowed in your family of origin. In your journal you may want to do some drawing, putting each character in your family in his or her own circle. Now draw lines between the characters to show how the communication generally flowed. In several families with whom I have worked, the mother was the center of all communication. If anyone had a question for another family member, Mother was the one to whom the question was directed.

2. Do the same exercise for your present family, but this time sit the entire family down for an evening, spread out a sheet of newsprint, and have family members diagram the communication patterns within the family. (Note: this exercise can be done with any group of people: church board, corporate structure, ball team and the like.)

3. Now think of how each character speaks with each other character in the family. Note the style that is used with each other character (placating, blaming, computer, distracting). You'll probably note that styles change as a character interacts with different other characters. (For example, "Mother is a placater with Father, a computer with me, a blamer with my older brother").

4. Next, look at the charts you have made of your family of origin and your current family. See if you can detect coalitions that were present—that is, family members who had joined with other family members for certain purposes. (For example, "Mom was mad at Dad but couldn't express it openly. So she formed a coalition with Sis, using Sis to fight with Dad and get her anger out by proxy.")

8
The
Story's
Setting

O*n the face of it the* Simmons family looked very typical of other suburban American families. And in many ways they *were* the typical family. They resided in the suburbs, in a neat two-story four-bedroom house on a cul-de-sac just down from a strip mall and the local elementary school. All the lawns in their neighborhood were well manicured. One never heard the sound of gunfire, and the squeal of tires was rare. Most people in the neighborhood went to church. Most people sent their children to college. And most people worked in white-collar jobs.

But there was more to this family than these externals. As members of the "Quiet" generation, Bill and Mary tended to be conservative and predictable. But other forces were obviously at work. Mary had been raised in a strict Greek Orthodox home. The church calendar provided the rhythm for all family events, and family loyalty was considered the supreme virtue. Family took precedence over all other considerations. Mary thus found herself torn between the needs of her husband and children and the demands of her parents and siblings, who seemed to call constantly to insist on one thing or another.

Bill's family, on the other hand, was not a factor at all in Bill and Mary's life. In fact, they tended to stay away too much, giving the impression that they didn't care.

The mood in Bill and Mary's home tended to shift between anger and sadness. Because Bill was a minister and the family was considered a model of family virtue, most often anger was driven underground, where it simmered unresolved. Replacing it was an overriding sadness, a quiet desperation, that seemed to permeate the household.

The Importance of Setting

Have you ever thought about the circumstances that surrounded your birth and upbringing? Have you considered what part of the country (or a foreign country) you were raised in and the influences this exerted on you? Many things were going on in the world when you were born—perhaps a world war, an extended time of peace, a civil upheaval, a famine—that influenced the ways your family story developed. These external elements of your family story, primarily the time and place of the story, constitute the *setting* of your story.

The importance of a family story's setting was brought home to me dramatically when I moved my family from northern Virginia to northern California some years back. On the face of it, very little seemed to have changed. Everyone spoke the same language, dressed more or less as we did, drove the same cars, used the same furniture. But over the first months that we were in our new home, differences began to emerge. There were little things (people used different colloquialisms, had dissimilar mannerisms) and not so little things (roads, which were in great shape, were given funding priority over schools, which were rotting down). The fact that we were in a whole new region of the country with new landscapes, climate, road systems (I kept getting lost driving home from work) and the like built up a particular mood within our family that in turn affected the way each of us felt about ourselves and our situation.

Setting forms the backdrop against which the family story emerges. Having talked to hundreds of families over the years, I have concluded that the best place to begin thinking about the setting of the family story is at the dinner table, with the family eating meals together.

In another family the father ate in the kitchen while the rest of the family ate in the dining room. Still other families never sat down together. But there are also families where there is lively and engrossing discussion, theological debate, the enjoyment and celebration of each other's individuality. Many families maintain ethnic distinctives and nurture cultural symbols that make dinnertime special.

On the face of things, my wife and I came from similar families. Both were solidly middle-class and Christian. Her mother and my father are both German in heritage. But I remember when I first went to visit her family and shared dinner with them. I was horrified. Their conversation during dinner was quiet and polite, with classical music playing in the background. My family, by contrast, horrified my wife. We all seemed to talk at once during dinner, the decibel level rising as the minutes passed. When a topic of conversation arose, everyone seemed to pounce on it like a pack of hungry wolves leaping on a stricken foe.

I've heard countless stories about dinnertime in various families. In one family the father ladled out the food, with the others' plates stacked in front of him. He determined who got how much. No one was allowed to talk during the meal. The only sound heard was chewing.

Exercise. The place to begin in exploring the role of setting in your family story is the dinner table. Think back to when you were growing up (if you are now grown), or your family story now, and imagine a typical scene at the dinner table. Notice who is there, who sits next to whom, who speaks to whom. Did everyone come to dinner? Is the atmosphere positive and upbeat or negative and depressing? Are there ethnic distinctives?

Write your observations in your journal. If you want to make this a family activity, spread out newsprint and draw a stick-figure rendition of dinnertime in your family of origin. Have each child draw his or her own impressions of what dinnertime is currently like for them.

What Is the Setting?
Matthew came from an Oregon family that valued self-sufficiency.

Everyone went their own way, did their own thing. His wife Sheila came from rural Appalachia; her forebears were coal miners of Scotch-Irish descent. Family was everything to her, and ways of carrying out family customs were laid out very specifically. To Matthew family was incidental. There were few rituals of import to his family. When his father died, the body was taken from the house, prepared, and buried in three days. When Sheila's father died, the whole community mourned for a week. The body was laid out in the church for three days, informal choirs formed as people came and went, and singing went on continually until after the viewing. Then members of the family went to the ancestral burial plot and hand-dug the grave. The funeral procession wove through town, stopping traffic.

Matthew had no sense at all of how his family stretched back through history. He had hardly known either set of grandparents. He barely knew the national origin of his surname. He did not know how his family had gotten to Oregon or the circumstances that led them there. Sheila knew great detail about both sides of her family generations back. The town in which she was raised was largely made up of relatives. The old women of the town would sit on their porches on hot summer afternoons and tells stories of the family. "You've got to know where you came from," her grandmother would remind her. "It lets you know who you are and where you came from."

Setting is not merely the physical backdrop of a story (the neighborhood, town, state and nation) but also historical background, cultural attitudes, the general inclination of thought or feeling characteristic of a particular period of time, the overall mood or *Zeitgeist*. Setting also involves the mood within a family which is established by outside factors (culture, historical background) and by the emotional life of the characters within the story.

Setting makes some things possible, other things impossible. Theologian J. I. Packer says that culture (which is a major part of setting) is "both binoculars and blinkers."[1] Culture helps you see some things yet keeps you from seeing other things.

Setting can be seen as the backbone of your story. It serves as a unifying factor in the unfolding story. In many ways, setting helps to shape who we are, how we think and feel, and how we respond to the myriad situations that confront us.

The Time Dimension of Setting

We have already explored the individual's and family's developmental march. But as the family is moving through its own unfolding story, society does not remain static. Each generation possesses a distinct sense of self, a peer personality manifesting certain collective behaviors, traits and attitudes, a core set of stories to which the people in that generation adhere. The movie *Forrest Gump* was very popular with baby boomers precisely because it detailed that generation's particular story setting and collective behavior.

William Strauss and Neil Howe, two writers and social commentators, have attempted to look at American history from the nation's inception to discover generational patterns through the centuries.[2] They found a recurring cycle of four distinct types (dominant type followed by recessive, followed in turn by another dominant and recessive, before the cycle begins again). Over U.S. history, Strauss and Howe found a correspondence between recurring patterns of generational "constellations" and recurring types of historical events. Each of the living generations in our society today bear a striking similarity to corresponding generations of the same type in the past.

The first dominant generation, the "idealists" or spiritual folks, ushered in the religious awakenings. The next dominant generation, called "civics" or nation builders, faced the great crises in our history (Revolution, Civil War, Depression and world war) and were able to shape our great institutions. Recessive generations between the dominant generations, though overshadowed by these, nonetheless have had their own particular distinctives. Following are summaries of the characteristics of the four generational types.

1. *Idealist* (dominant): *the Spiritual generations.* These generations grew up as indulged youths after the great secular crises (wars and depressions) of history. As they matured, these generations turned

inward, inspiring the great spiritual awakenings that have transformed the nation every eighty or so years. These are the moralizing generations of Susan B. Anthony and Henry David Thoreau, stretching back to the Great Awakenings, missionary movements and revivals of Jonathan Edwards, D. L. Moody and Charles Finney. These generations trigger cultural creativity and challenge the values that have been foundational to older institutions.

The current baby boomers are members of this idealist type. Back during the sixties and early seventies, as these young boomers came to maturity, they embarked on an inward search to find meaning in their existence. Whether individually or banded together in informal communes, the boomers focused on self. Boomers became the antithesis to the previous generation: "spiritualism over science, gratification over patience, negativism over positivism, fractiousness over conformity, rage over friendliness, self over community."[4]

As children were born to them, these children were often left to raise themselves while Mom and Dad pursued inward journeys that led from the mysticism of India and exotic Asian spiritualities back to our shores and adventures found in drugs and sex.

2. *Reactive* (recessive): *the Lost generations.* These children have grown up as underprotected and criticized youths during spiritual awakenings (their parents are out seeking spiritual experiences and have no time for them). They mature into risk-taking, alienated young adults, strongly desiring early independence. Later they mellow into pragmatic midlife leaders during secular crises. Finally, in the twilight of life, they maintain respect (but less influence) as reclusive adults. As confidence in institutions declines, individualism flourishes.

Members of Generation X, those among us born between roughly 1962 and 1982, are part of this generation. This generation is less idealistic than their baby boomer parents. To Xers the world is a difficult and complex place. One must play by whatever rules needed to survive. There is little tolerance for anything that smacks of "the system." Boomers questioned the system. Xers avoid it.

Xers grew up with little or no familial support. Consequently they look for a sense of community wherever they can find it. Friends and relationships are extremely important, though there is confusion in this generation as to what healthy relationship really is. They want friends who will be loyal. Their parents expressed moral ambivalence where Xers sought clear answers, hesitated to impose structure on their children's behavior, and demonstrated an amazing tolerance for the rising torrent of pathology and negativism that engulfed their children's world.

This is the first generation in American history, social analyst George Barna reminds us, that has not begun its spiritual pilgrimage with Christianity.[3] Having been exposed through the media to a myriad of spiritual options, Xers have moved down numerous paths in their quest for fulfillment.

3. *Civic* (dominant): *the Nation Builders*. These children have grown up as increasingly protected youths after spiritual awakenings. They come of age overcoming a secular crisis. They then unite into a heroic and achieving cadre of rising adults facing social peril. They build institutions to overcome the dangers they have faced. Self-discovery is sacrificed on the altar of teamwork. They emerge as busy elders attacked by the next generation in the unfolding spiritual awakenings.

The G.I. generation that ushered in the New Deal and then World War II are part of this generational type still alive. All their lives they have placed a high value on being regular. They value the outer life over the inner life favored by boomers. Their message is "Don't tell me what you're thinking, show me what you're doing." Their optimistic energy to do was channeled into group activities, into harmonious community, into government building. They have expected to wield their powers and see progress. This generation has expected much from government and stares in disbelief as boomers now stand ready to dismantle all the government systems put in place by this generation.

4. *Adaptive* (recessive): *the Silent generations*. These children grow up as overprotected, suffocated youths during depressions and wars.

They mature into risk-averse adults who are ready to conform. As they grow older, indecision seems to be a hallmark. These generations seem to find themselves missing out on all the action—either twenty years too early for the self-absorbed spiritual generation or twenty years too late for the get-it-done civic and social crowd. Attention has always tended to be focused on another generation, so this generation was content to remain silent and not make too many waves.

Those born between 1925 and 1945 who are currently in places of leadership throughout the country are part of this generation. They have not been risk-takers. They have largely been cautious, unimaginative and unadventurous. As they moved into the work force, they preferred job security in large corporations and government. They have largely been affluent, have been able to live amidst relative national tranquillity, and as a result have suffered less of the social pathologies (crime, suicide, teen unemployment) that other generations have lamented.

When the Silent Generation appealed for change, they didn't spin into an angry fury but rather invoked the basic humanity and social conscience of the nation.

Childrearing Through the Generations

The way children are perceived and treated has followed generational constellations. It has also shaped each generation's peer personality.

Lost generations have always been children at the worst possible times. These folks were born during the great spiritual awakening years, when parents were more concerned about themselves, their own spiritual welfare and the need to dismantle elder-built institutions. Lost Generation children were left largely to raise themselves. While Silent generations mediated between the Spirituals and the Nation Builders, the Lost generations were left to look on in dismay. This is the major difference we are currently seeing between Generation X (those who seem to be committed to nothing) and the boomers who raised them, the flower children of the sixties.

During years when war and pestilence stalk the land and the *Nation Builders* are parents, these opposites to the Spiritual parents produce the opposite form of nurture: suffocating overprotection of Silent (adaptive) children. Nation Builder generations exalt family and community over the self (and one's inner spiritual needs). The home is assiduously guarded. Children are denied independence or adventure as they come of age. They're told to behave, be quiet and be thankful to their elders for sacrifices on their behalf. So where the Spiritual generations tend to underprotect, the Nation Builders tend to overprotect their children.

The dominant generational types spend their childhoods midway between extremes of over- and underprotection. Nation Builders grow up during eras when adult control is increasing. Spiritual generations grow up when adult control is decreasing.

Generations tend to raise their children in a manner *opposite* the way in which they themselves were raised. Parents produce overprotected kids, who in turn raise underprotected kids. A generation raised under tightening parental grip relax that grip when they in turn become parents; their chldren retighten the grip with their own offspring.

The Dimension of Place

Steve was raised in rural Wisconsin on a dairy farm. Marta hails from a Mexican enclave in East Los Angeles. Jerome comes from public housing on the west side of Chicago. Michelle comes from the affluent suburbs of Atlanta. Each of these young people grew up in America, but the places in which they grew are as different as any place on earth.

We think of the various regions of the United States—the Deep South, the Far West, the Northeast, the Midwest—as distinct environments. But within regions there are also vast distinctions. An inner-city dweller may find she has little in common with a kid who lives ten miles away in the suburbs. A boy on the farm has a different experience from one who is raised down the road in a small town.

The dimension of place also includes special objects that represent important memories to us. First is the family dwelling, the particular architecture and surrounding landscape of that dwelling. Within the dwelling are the particular articles that make that home unique.

As I glance around my house (a two-story colonial painted gray-brown), I see the antique chest of drawers with a marble top that Marcy and I bought the first year we were married. We weren't necessarily looking for antiques. We just wanted furniture we could afford, and twenty-five years ago, old furniture (a.k.a. antique) was the least expensive kind. We traveled out into the countryside of Virginia and came upon a house where a little old man displayed on the porch several pieces of old furniture he himself had finished. We chose the chest.

Almost any object in our home has a story attached to it: the M-1 Grandpa carried in the Great War, the knitting needles Mom used to make my quilt, the jewelry, the pictures, the old toys. Some items have what we call sentimental value because the attached story is so meaningful to the family story. I've been in countless homes where after I begin to examine an object, the owner comes and tells me its special story.

Often such objects are tied to the family myths and therefore take on particularly powerful meanings to the family. Other objects directly correlate to the family premise or are significant in the unfolding family plot.

Exercise. Set aside the book and take a moment to think of the dwelling in which you were raised. What made it distinctive in appearance? Now think of one or two objects that are important to you in your current home. What story do you tell when you're asked about the object? See if you can tie the object to themes discussed in this book: family myths or secrets, the family premise, the development of your character.

The Ethnic Dimension

Though I was born into a family that had some ethnic diversity, we were somewhat "vanilla" in comparison to others I have since met

who were raised amid much greater ethnic variety. My father, born in
Germany, had come to the United States before World War I. Because
of anti-German sentiment, he and his family had largely forsaken their
German heritage. My mother came from Scotch-Irish and English
descendants who had come to northern Virginia in the late 1600s and
stayed put for generations. Over the years, people from many other
areas had come to northern Virginia to work in Washington, D.C.
Consequently the area had lost real regional distinctives. When I was
growing up, there was nothing distinctly German or even Scotch-Irish
to distinguish our family from any other suburban family of the fifties.

When I became an adult, I traced my mother's family back through
the generations in northern Virginia, following my great-grandfather
through the Civil War and my great-great-great-great-grandfather
through the American Revolution. Now I have the desire to go back
to Germany and piece together my father's family story, to determine
who these people were and what particular influences surrounded their
lives.

The setting of our family story includes the critical element of
ethnicity. Nations have different personalities shaped by climate, heat,
light, moisture, quality of the soil, food, history, customs, religions,
even fears and guilt feelings. National personalities shape resident
peoples and create ethnic distinctives. As these peoples have come to
American shores, many of these ethnic distinctives have survived,
albeit in modified form.

Ethnicity gives us the power of group identity and belonging. If you
were raised in a community with a strong ethnic identity, that identity
was deeply ingrained in your personal story, in addition to your
developing family story. Within this community you were able to
relax, secure in the knowledge that you shared the same window on
the world and basically saw the world in similar ways as your
neighbors.

How people left their native shores to come to America, how they
went about making that decision (or were forced to leave, as were
African-Americans), what emotional ties were maintained and sev-

ered—all contribute to the ways in which people adjusted to their new surroundings and to what degree they maintained cultural distinctives.

But hailing from a distinctly ethnic setting may not always be a benefit. Certain ethnic groups in our culture are celebrated. Others are ignored or even demeaned. Many immigrants have felt the sting of prejudice. To counter prejudice, many families edited out most ethnic distinctives from their family story. As a consequence, many people suffer the loss of an important element in their personal identity. Certainly the "melting pot" of the American culture caused all immigrants, to a greater or lesser degree, to sacrifice parts of their ethnic identity.

Many people, in considering their family story, have found it important to reconnect with their ethnic heritage, to mine the rich resources left behind in past generations. Traditions can be unearthed and brought back to life at holidays and special celebrations. Learning of our ethnic backgrounds puts us in touch with the larger stories from which our own family story has sprung. *Roots* is Alex Haley's moving account tracing his slave ancestry back to West Africa and finally to his family's home village and the tribal storyteller (griot), who pieced together his family story as it had been passed down orally over the centuries.[5]

Some couples find that differences in ethnic backgrounds have caused a great deal of conflict and grief in their marriage. The pull of opposing backgrounds can be intense, with in-laws lining up to fuel the inevitable conflicts. It becomes critical for these couples to decide that their marriage and family story is a priority, that family-of-origin stories must take a subordinate position. Further, the couple must develop good negotiating skills so that they are able to work through the disagreements that inevitably arise around customs, values and everyday living practices.

Some people were born to American parents but were raised in other cultures; examples are missionary kids and foreign service children. Having spent significant time growing up in another culture, they often borrow elements of that culture and mix it with their native

culture to make a third culture. These folks have come to be known
as "third-culture kids." If you are one of these, you probably already
realize that you think and function a little differently from your
contemporaries who were raised in America. Several positive and
negative characteristics of third-culture kids have been noted. On the
positive side . . .

☐ They're adept at least one other language.

☐ They have good crosscultural skills. They take time to observe a
situation before acting.

☐ Having observed a situation, they are good at discovering how to
fit in without necessarily compromising values.

☐ Their worldview is broader than that of people who grew up
monoculturally.

☐ Their view of God is larger than that of monocultural kids.

☐ They tend to be more mature.

However, there can be drawbacks:

☐ Third-culture kids often feel rootless, unable to identify with any
one culture.

☐ They are insecure in relationships, feeling none lasts very long.
They tend to form intense relationships quickly.

☐ They tend to be lonely, because of tenuous relationships and not
feeling a part of the culture where they reside.

☐ They feel off-balance, sensing that there's something they ought to
know but don't; they're always a little out of sync with the culture.

Exercise. Answer the following questions in your journal. You may
wish to talk to members of your immediate family or other relatives
to discover relevant details.

1. When and under what circumstances did your families come to
this country? (For example, "My parents were brought here as
slaves.")

2. Do you know the particular ethnic distinctives and traditions
from which your father and mother's family stories sprang? (For
example, "My mother was from a Polish Catholic family that was
extremely religious. A sense of family was very important to her.

My father was from a Reformed Jewish family that had largely forsaken ethnic distinctives. Family was less important to him.")

3. How have ethnic distinctives affected the development of your family story? (For example, "The Chinese New Year was the biggest celebration of the year. We prepared special foods, and the whole family gathered to celebrate.")

The Emotional Dimension

The mood in every story is critical, for it sets the tone for all that happens. Mood is the predominant feeling state of a story, the primary emotional set, and every family story has a particular mood. The mood could be joyfulness, sadness, fear (dread), anger, hopefulness, despair or boundless optimism. If you think of families you know, you can probably make a statement about the mood that seems to predominate in each of them. Mood can even be reflected in the colors people choose in their home furnishings: a preponderance of white suggests guilt; red suggests anger; green is peaceful, yellows express warmth; blue suggests sadness.

The overriding mood of the family story affects the emotional life of each character within the story. And the emotional life of each story character in turn affects the mood of that story. Mood reinforces the characters' feelings, and characters' feelings reinforce the story's mood. Examples of family moods are given in table 6.

Mood shifts have a way of heightening tension within a family. This is especially true when the shifts are not recognized, acknowledged and allowed for. Many families have trouble expressing and dealing with certain mood states. This happens when the parents have each had trouble with a particular feeling and then bring this difficulty into the marriage. Their inability to deal with the feeling is then passed on to their children.

The Simmons family, for example, had great difficulty dealing with anger. Bill's family had pushed anger under the carpet and never spoke of it. Mary's family let anger have free rein, which frightened all the children. Neither Bill nor Mary knew how to express anger positively,

	Slight	Moderate	Intense	Extreme
Sadness	disappointed	dejected	sorrowful	desolated
	wistful	despondent	mournful	anguished
Fear	uneasy	anxious	dreading	terrified
	worried	frightened	panicked	apprehensive
Aversion	dislike	repugnance	contempt	abhorrence
	disrespect	disdain	disgust	loathing
Anger	frustrated	resentful	bitter	raging
	annoyed	indignant	wrathful	furious
Guilt	regretful	repentant	remorseful	self-hating
	sheepish	contrite	reprehensible	self-flagellating
Joy	cheerful	glad	elated	blissful
	contented	delighted	exhilarated	ecstatic

Table 6. Moods of the family[6]

so these parents never expressed anger. Daughter Julie never expressed anger either (and ended up with gastrointestinal problems). Marie expressed her anger indirectly, by acting out sexually. Billy expressed his anger in a direct, hostile way (and to a degree he seemed to express the collective anger of the family), staying angry all the time about everything and everyone.

The Religious Dimension: Loss of the Christian Mind
In recent generations we in the West have experienced profound cultural shifts that have profoundly affected the church. The complexity of cultural currents that have swirled around the church and the family story have left many Christians bewildered. Recently a number of fine books and articles have examined these trends quite thoroughly. Here I wish to make note of several of these trends as they affect the unfolding family story.

Noted Christian writer and thinker Os Guinness has suggested that over the years there was a retreat from the Christian mind, with a concurrent rise of a diluted mind. The Puritans had established a colony based on the mind. Every aspect of their existence was carefully thought out to ensure biblical conformity. Gradually that mindset was eroded or "hollowed out." Several powerful influences rushed in to fill the void and have affected our ability to think with the mind of Christ. Not surprisingly, these influences mirror current trends in our culture.[7]

Polarization. The Puritans maintained a magnificent balance between worship and learning, theology and experience. Over the years Christians have polarized into those who are fervent in worship, stressing experience, and those who seek to improve their minds and dig deeply into theology.

Pietism. A bare subjectivism has developed which is cut off from theology. This has brought on a shift from theology to experience and an antitheological state of mind among Christians.

Primitivism. American experience has generally favored the primitive. To be American was to be ex-European, getting back to a lost innocence. This left people with a bias against tradition, institution, the settled, the elaborated. Evangelicals now have an enormous impatience with anything difficult to think through. They want the simple, the simplistic, that which is quickly understood.

Populism. The right to personal judgment became the Magna Carta of the common man. This led to an orientation that is anti-authoritarian, antitraditional and radically individual. The result, in turn, has been a leveling of any sense of truth, discipline, experience and maturity.

Pluralism. Pluralism is our consciousness that there are many more options for ultimate faith commitments available to us than we had been accustomed to. It is a social phenomenon and doesn't necessarily lead to any particular set of convictions. Plurality itself isn't bad. The fledgling church flourished in the pluralism of Roman and Greek cultures. But increasingly the pluralistic makeup of society, combined with other shifts, has propelled people to embrace the philosophy of relativism.

Relativism is the belief that all moral, philosophical and religious positions are the product of someone's personal, subjective understanding. It is the commonly expressed belief that there are many valid views on any subject. Relativism makes it easier for folks of differing worldviews to tolerate each other. If you're a true relativist, it really doesn't matter what anyone thinks. Taken to an extreme, however, relativism becomes another doctrine positing absolutes. Ironically, the primary absolute is there are no absolutes (which is paradoxical and absurd).

Within the church, people often put the most demanding parts of their beliefs behind their backs, as it were, and highlight only the most appealing aspects of the faith. Eventually, in a desire to offend no one and to win everyone, there is an indifference to truth.

Pragmatism. Tradition has been devalued in American culture. Instead a premium is put on hard work, ingenuity, common sense and know-how. Theology tends to soften into technique. Serving God becomes servicing the self. Knowing in whom to believe becomes knowing how to do things. Faith in God becomes faith in faith, or positive thinking.

Because Western Christians are losing (or have lost) a Christian mindset, it is critical that we begin to reacquaint ourselves with the truths of our faith. Not having a solid Christian mind as each of us writes our story leaves us vulnerable to the negative influences of the surrounding setting. Christian truths need to inform every aspect of our unfolding stories. Genuine understanding will generate genuine faith, which in turn will generate genuine experience.

The Religious Dimension: Loss of Significant Relationships
Deeply ingrained individualism lies behind much contemporary understanding of love and community. In today's climate the individual decides what he wants, then finds relationships that fulfill his needs. People were created for lasting relationships, but in our culture relationships (be they marriage, friendship, church or business relationships) may last only so long as they fill the individual's needs. Love becomes no more than a utilitarian exchange: I get

what I want, you get what you want.

Loss of marriage and family. Much has been written about the loss of family relationships. At the base of these relationships is promise. It seems as though people generally, and even people within the Christian community, have had a difficult time of late keeping their most important promises to one another.

Loss of close friendships. With increasing mobility and the attendant isolation, people no longer experience the deep, lasting friendships that older generations relied on to stabilize their sense of self and community. There have also been a loss of accountability relationships, which have historically been critical in averting moral failings.

Loss of community. As this trend emerges in Christian circles, it reflects trends in the wider culture. Instead of community, people have moved into lifestyle enclaves, expressions of private tastes linked closely to leisure and consumption.[8] People with this way of life find it hard to be consistent, for they constantly long for a larger commitment and obligation that would go beyond personal need. It is critical that the church demonstrate agape love in the reawakening and unfolding of Christian community.

What Should I Do About the Effects of Setting on My Story?

Ancient Near Eastern settings form the backdrop of the unfolding biblical story of redemption. The Bible is concerned with places as well as events. Great care is given to anchor events in place and time. Jesus came to this earth, to a particular country, during a particular era, and immersed himself in the culture of his day.

The Bible includes numerous examples of people who grew up experiencing in a particular setting but transcended that setting to do mighty things. Moses radically altered his setting twice. He was raised in the courts of the most powerful nation of his time. Then he was in a desert for forty years chasing sheep. Finally he walked in front of his people as he led them through the desert. David was a poet and a shepherd. Gideon and Amos were from insignificant families.

The different writing styles of the authors of the New Testament generally reflect the settings from which these people sprang. Luke, a physician, had an excellent command of Greek word usage and made good use of metaphor. His Gospel flows elegantly. Peter, by contrast, was a semiliterate fisherman. His writing style is simple and direct. These men came from completely different backgrounds. God did not set aside these differences so that each man could appear as a mirror of the other.

Many of the effects of setting on your life do not need to be altered. In fact, you can rejoice in many aspects of your story's setting. Yet we also realize that as a Christian people, we must be somewhat cautious regarding various aspects of our setting, realizing that we can be molded into attitudes, ideas and postures that run contrary to God's call on us (Rom 12:2).

Evangelical elder statesman John Stott spoke eloquently to this point in an interview: "One of the great barriers to our understanding the Word of God is our own cultural defenses. If we're not careful, all we will hear in our Bible reading are the echoes of our own cultural prejudices. We need to cry to God to break through our biases." Stott went on to recommend that every Christian become an internationalist, contacting and discovering peoples from other cultures in whatever ways are available, making sure that the gospel is seen in light of the larger Story of what God has been doing through the ages and through many cultures.[9]

There are three key elements to the process of gaining perspective on our culture.

1. *Inventory.* Begin to notice, and to discuss with friends, how culture permeates your life. Notice your home, your dress, the magazines, cars and other objects that fill your life. Take careful notice of advertisements on TV. Note the cultural distinctives in them, and the subtle messages they give.

2. *Involvement.* Get involved with people of another culture. Invite exchange and foreign students to your home for meals. Learn of their culture and customs. Visit or get involved in ministries that work with

different segments of our own culture (for example, if you live in the suburbs, learn more about the inner-city church). You may want to make another culture a project with your children. The whole family can support a child through a Christian relief organization. You can also adopt a missionary family, writing to them and learning all about the culture they are in. You can get old *National Geographic* magazines and cut out pictures from the country you are focusing on.

3. *Insight.* We must be sure that when we speak of God's Story, we are accurately telling that Story and not adding our own cultural accoutrements. Sit down with missionaries home on furlough and discuss with them how they approach cultural questions where they minister. In your small group discuss how the American way and the Christian way have become intertwined. Begin to develop strategies to disengage the gospel from those parts of the culture that are destructive to its message.

Begin to note your own and your family's lifestyle. What do you spend your time and money on? (For example, "I get a new car every two years. I've been influenced by my culture to drive a new car as a symbol of status. I no longer see a car as merely a means of transportation.") You may want to begin to develop goals and objects for bringing your lifestyle more in line with kingdom principles, not cultural mandates.

Exercises. These exercises will help you explore the particular elements of setting that have been operating as your family story has unfolded: time, place and outlook.

Exercise 1. Begin to construct in your journal a picture of the time in which you were born. You might do any of the following:

☐ Get a copy of *Life* magazine for the month you were born. Notice what was happening then, what fashions were in style, what the mood of the country was.

☐ Note the particular generational time in which you were born and its characteristics. The following summary is adapted from *Generations.*

Cycle	Generation	Type	Birth years	Sample members
Great power	Missionary	Idealist	1860-1882	F. D. Roosevelt
	Lost	Reactive	1883-1900	Dwight Eisenhower
	G.I.	Civic	1901-1924	John Kennedy
	Silent	Adaptive	1925-1942	Walter Mondale
Millennial	Boom	Idealist	1943-1960	Bill Clinton
	Generation X	Reactive	1961-1981	Tom Cruise
	Millennial	Civic (?)	1982-	Jessica McClure

Note the particular distinctives of your generation as described earlier in this chapter. What particular distinctives of your generation have affected the way you think and act? Journal your perceptions.

□ Initiate a discussion with your family of origin regarding any particular cultural distinctives that were present in your family as you were growing up. Gather any genealogical information you can find, and chart your family tree over several generations. Find out what you can about when your family first came to America (provided you are not a Native American). See if you can find out the impact that immigration (or forced importation if your ancestors came in bondage) had on your family.

□ Take out the time line of your unfolding family story which you created earlier. See if you can identify the various moods that predominated in your family story at critical moments in the story.

Exercise 2. Write in your journal a short description of the physical setting in which you were raised. Recall the street, the neighborhood, the small town, suburb or inner city. What particular aspects stand out in your mind (the trees, the corner grocery, the constantly barking dogs)? As an alternative, draw a picture, a diagram or a map of the area in which you were raised.

Exercise 3. Identify the particular mood that seems to predominate in your family-of-origin story. You may want to discuss how the mood changed during unfolding chapters of the story. (For example, "When I first went off to elementary school, the mood in our household was depressed. When I reached adolescence, the mood had changed to guarded optimism.")

Next list several feelings in your journal, leaving a space under each. Then write how your family handled each of these as they arose.

Sadness

Fear

Aversion

Anger

Guilt

Joy

9
The
Ongoing
Story

I *worked with the* Simmons family for a number of months. I was thankful that each family member proved willing to come, to talk and to take responsibility for him- or herself (though this took some time to achieve for young Billy, and also for Marie, who tended to feel like the family victim). Family members began to see the roles they had assumed with each other as the family story unfolded. Negative patterns of dialogue were identified and eliminated. Mary learned to talk to Marie about her own out-of-wedlock pregnancy and her fears that her daughter would follow in her footsteps.

Bill and Mary learned how to deal with each other more effectively and create more positive moments for each other, thus strengthening their leadership function in the family. They began to see how they had undercut each other's authority over the years, which led to a great deal of confusion in the family. And generally, the family agreed to continue to work hard to be for each other and for themselves what God had originally created them to be.

Though the Simmons family story continues to unfold, as does the individual story of each family member, there had been resolution of the major crises that first brought them to my attention.

By now we've explored the many facets of the family story. We've looked at how parents first wrote that story, the elements they drew upon to create the story in all its uniqueness. We looked at how characters were fashioned and introduced into the story, how the premise of the story led to its overall design and how the plot has unfolded over time. Our goal is to achieve quality stories, not pulp fiction. We want the characters in our stories to have substance, to have depth and to be virtuous. We want the plot to unfold in ways that will be beneficial to all the characters, and ultimately pleasing to God.

Before you go through this final chapter, take out your journal and review all the different parts you have written. If you haven't been journaling, think back on the different elements of story we've covered and how each has affected you. You should have examined your family of origin, your role in that family story and how your character was shaped through the years. You should also have written about your present family story and your personal story.

Your last exercise in this book is divided into several parts. It will help you synthesize your material, bringing your personal story and your family story into one distinct story. You may find it easier to write the two stories separately and integrate them later. If you have been telling the parts of your story to someone else, go back to your friend to put your story together. Later you'll have a chance to consider how the story is to be written in the future.

Our Personal Story

As I finish this book, I am well into my forty-ninth year. My individual story has progressed into midlife. I have weathered several midlife complications: we moved to California and back again, my mother became ill and died, two of my children have left home for college and beyond. When I was twenty-one I could never have guessed any of my story to this point. At that age I was engaged to be married. I had a vague idea about being a counselor of some sort. But I was up to my ears in youth work and had not yet finished my undergraduate degree, and the paths I would take were in no way clear.

My story has included my marriage to Marcy and my progress through graduate school as I worked in public mental health. It has included the birth of our three children, and the presence of other characters who have moved into and out of my life. Complications have arisen, from minor interruptions and upsets to more substantial changes: our move to California, new jobs, the illness and death of loved ones.

My wife and I now are watching our nest empty. For the first time since the earliest years of our marriage we are able to do spontaneous things together without the fear of leaving children unsupervised. I am turning more of my attention to writing and am wondering about the next chapters in my story.

Look at each element of your own story, so that you are sure you include in your narrative the most important aspects:

☐ What chapter of my life's story am I in? What are the specific challenges I am facing at this chapter in my personal story?

☐ What does my character look like at this point? What do I really value? What burns at the core of my being as the most important elements of my life? What are my gifts? my talents? What do I like to do? with whom? when?

☐ What roles do I play, and in what settings?

☐ What is the premise of my story?

☐ What have been the major features of my personal story's plot line?

☐ What have been the distinctive aspects of its setting?

Write as much or as little as you like. Try to tell your personal story as you understand it today.

Family Story

The family story unfolds concurrently with my personal story (as do many other stories—cultural, business, national, church and so on). The patterns are the same as in the personal story, though the emphasis is slightly different. Now write, or narrate, your unfolding family story using the elements below.

☐ What chapter is my family now in? How successful have we been up to this point in writing the earlier chapters of our family story?

☐ What are the particular challenges our family faces during this chapter?

☐ Who are the particular characters in our family story?

☐ What roles does each character play?

☐ What is the particular quality of the dialogue in the family story? Who talks to whom? about what? when?

☐ What elements of the story's setting are particularly important?

☐ What have been the most important elements in the unfolding plot (complications, antagonists, important scenes)?

Into the Future

In the letter to the Philippians, St. Paul described the Christian's orientation perfectly: "Forgetting what is behind and straining toward what is ahead, I press on toward the goal to win the prize for which God has called me heavenward in Christ Jesus" (3:13-14). Paul knew that our orientation is to live today *out of the future.* We must not be paralyzed with "if onlys," as in "if only I'd been born in a different family," "if only I'd had fewer complications to face" or "if only I'd had a different setting."

Our frame of reference, the criterion by which we examine everything we do and say, must be what we see at the end of our life, the goal toward which we are striving. I'm told that athletes training for the Olympics, rising before sunup and working hour after hour, day after day, keep before them the image of themselves standing on the platform, the gold medal around their necks, the national anthem sounding over loudspeakers. That's the goal, and it is this they keep foremost in their mind, not the defeats and failures they have endured in the past.

This is not to say that we can just turn off the past as if we were switching off a TV set. We have all suffered various complications that have left their marks on our lives. But our stories have not unfolded without meaning or purpose. We are shaping and being shaped by the true Storyteller, who desires to work us into his story in ways that will ultimately turn out for the good.

So we now think of the future. What do we want our stories to look like in the years ahead? I'm told that stories can be written in two ways. The author can envision several characters, put them in a particular setting and then let the action unfold, following along in her mind as she writes. The other way to write is to sit down and outline a plan for the story, to begin with the end in view. I personally prefer this second approach. However, most people I talk to use the first approach—letting life unfold with no particular plan in mind.

Set the book down and take several minutes for this exercise (which was adapted from Stephen Covey's *The Seven Habits of Highly Effective People.*[1] Close your eyes and imagine yourself at your own funeral. You lie in the casket. Your family and friends have assembled in the chapel and now face your casket. Look at the program for the service. There are four speakers. One is from your family, one is a close friend, one is from work, and one is from your church. Think deeply now about what you would like these four speakers to say about you. What were you like as a father/husband/brother or mother/wife/sister? What were you like as a friend?

One of the most challenging aspects of writing your personal story, and especially your family story (if you are now married), is the need to collaborate with a cowriter. On two occasions I wrote a book with my friend Jim Denney, a seasoned writer. I supplied him with raw material, and he fashioned each sentence (unlike this book, in which I have done the fashioning and the editors at InterVarsity Press have done the polishing). When I write my personal story, hopefully I collaborate with God in following his original story line. When my wife Marcy and I write our family story, ideally I collaborate with her and with God in fashioning an appropriate story.

Collaboration involves several elements:

☐ *Good communication.* Unfortunately, little of what I have spoken of in this book is readily understood by the average couple. Couples don't tend to be aware of the need to communicate about premise or character development or plot. The family story just unfolds of its own accord, without direction or forethought.

Spouses who are cowriting a family story need to be able to speak clearly and congruently to each other. They must be able to talk about the issues that are the most important in writing a clear, concise, biblically grounded story.

□ *Common goals.* Begin with the end in view, as Stephen Covey states. Agree first on what is deeply important to both of you. Set these elements as the goal of the story. Then outline the story and determine the destination before actually beginning to write.

This approach is appealing and helpful, but it is not without danger. It is critical that I learn to set goals with my spouse for our family story and work toward those goals. But it is also critical that I realize that as the story unfolds, complications will undoubtedly arise to thwart my goals and lead me down paths that I never anticipated.

□ *The ability to negotiate.* If I want my way all the time with no qualifications, I will be in deep trouble when it comes to collaboration. By any means necessary, I will put my energy into trying to get my way. The most productive approach, however, is the "win/win" policy. Here my chief concern is to achieve mutual benefit to myself *and* my spouse. I am not merely struggling to have my own way.

Realize, though that you and your cowriter will never achieve consensus on everything that has happened in your family story. There are at least three different stances people take as they seek to understand their family stories:[2]

1. *Traditionalists.* These folks think almost everything that happened in their family-of-origin story was excellent, and they want very much to continue that story. Often the negative elements of the story are denied (which means that these are likely to pop up again in the current family story).

2. *Rebels.* These people basically despise everything that has happened and seek to write the exact opposite family story. However, as the rebel inadvertently repeats despised patterns, the past is often repeated by default.

3. *Synthesizers.* The synthesizers pick and choose what parts of the

past family story they want to repeat and what parts they want to eliminate. They see the unfolding family story as a process and are willing to make adjustments as changing circumstances dictate. They look at the past realistically, understanding the strengths and weaknesses of their family stories. These folks are best able then to set realistic goals for the future writing of their stories, borrowing liberally from elements that have worked in the past while laying to rest elements that have been faulty.

It may be helpful now to consolidate all your thoughts on your personal and family stories by making a chart like the one below. At a glance you'll be able to see what changes you need to make and what areas will remain the same.

Think of your story and the assessment you've made of it, and see if you can divide its elements into two parts. Parts of the story cannot change. The experiences you've already had cannot change. They happened in the past; they're over and cannot be altered. Something that *can* change, however, is my *perspective* on what happened. I can look at my experiences with different eyes, as Joseph did in Genesis 50:20.

Things I can change	Things I cannot change

And now for the goals, beginning with your personal story.

☐ What kind of character do I want to be? What needs to be at the center of my life? What practical steps should I now be taking to achieve this?

☐ How do I need to modify the premise of my personal story?

☐ In what ways can I prepare myself for complications that will arise in my unfolding plot?

☐ What changes do I need to make in my setting?

Continue with goals for your family story with your cowriter, if you have one.

☐ How do we want each of our children to develop? Allowing for their differences, what practical steps do we need to be taking to achieve these goals?

☐ How do we need to modify the premise of the family story?

☐ In what ways can we prepare ourselves for complications that will arise in our unfolding plot?

☐ What changes do we need to make in the setting of the story?

These final questions are merely a guide. You will probably find it helpful to set aside time to set goals for yourself and for your family once a year. Stephen Covey's *The Seven Habits of Highly Effective People* can be an excellent resource for continuing this process. And for now, a few final exercises will aid you in tying up any loose ends.

Conclusion

You've now completed this workbook, and in so doing you've hopefully been able to more fully grasp the forces that have been powerfully at work in your life, shaping you into the person you are today. I hope you have also gained some insights and tools that will assist you in the future as you seek to conform your story to the contours that God intends.

I encouraged you to journal or make some other meaningful record of these exercises. I hope that will become the basis of an ongoing record of your unfolding story.

There have undoubtedly been areas in your personal story and family story that you have wanted to change, areas that have been unhelpful or even destructive over the years. Most of us want changes to occur quickly. But keep in mind that change often takes a long time to unfold. Steady dedication to living according to the commitments you have now made, with the help of the Holy Spirit, plus consistent accountability is the formula that will help you achieve your goals.

Exercise 1. It's time to complete the genogram you've been drawing of your whole family. Try to extend it through several generations. You may need to contact relatives to get the correct information. Use this exercise to look at the unique contributions that each of these people made to your life. Also take a last look at any remaining trouble spots, with a view toward one last rewrite of your family story.

Exercise 2. If you have reasonably good relationships with the rest of your family—either family of origin or the family you have created with your spouse—schedule a family session to think through the various elements of story discussed in this book. If the family is gathering for Christmas or another holiday or function, you may want to ask each member to read this book and complete the exercises so that the family as a whole can discuss the family story.

This need not be a time of confrontation and conflict. If you want, you can make it fun. Provide large sheets of paper and have everyone draw scenes of Christmases gone by. Or ask them to talk about pleasant memories. Then you can lead into talking about roles in the family, the family premise and how the plot has unfolded over the years.

Many of the psalms recount how God led the children of Israel during the great epochs of national history. You may want to do the same, encouraging your family, as it unfolds its story, to see how God has led all of you, even in the complications of life.

Exercise 3. Turn to Scripture and see how the family stories of the people of God unfolded. This would be a good exercise for a Sunday-school class or Bible study. I've listed biblical family stories in two categories: those that provide only a partial glimpse and those that are fully developed over a period of time. Work through each family story, noting and describing the characters, the chapters, the premise, the dialogue patterns and the plot. Notice how God used the family story to shape the individual characters.

Glimpses of family stories

Adam and Eve: Genesis 2—4

Noah: Genesis 5—9

Ruth: book of Ruth

Elkanah and Hannah: 1 Samuel 1—2

Gideon: Judges 6

Samson: Judges 13—16

For further study, go through the books of the Kings and Chronicles, then through the prophets, and note the impact of family on the various characters in these accounts.

Full family portraits

Abraham and Sarah (note how themes begun in this family will repeat through generations): Genesis 12—23

Isaac and Rebekah (note how the parents choose favorites among the children): Genesis 24—27

Jacob and Rachel/Leah (note sibling rivalry, stepfamily difficulty): Genesis 27—50

Moses: Exodus

Saul: 1 Samuel 9—31

David: 1 Samuel 16—2 Samuel

Notes

Introduction
[1] R. C. Schank, *Tell Me a Story* (New York: Scribner's, 1990), p. 12.
[2] Leighton Ford, *The Power of Story* (Colorado Springs, Colo.: NavPress, 1994), pp. 76-77.

Chapter 1: A Well-Written Story
[1] Werner Neuer, *Man and Woman in Christian Perspective* (Wheaton, Ill.: Crossway, 1991), p. 31.
[2] Bill Richie, *A Dad Who Loves You* (Portland, Ore.: Multnomah Press, 1992), p. 155.
[3] Neuer, *Man and Woman,* p. 72.
[4] Christopher Bollas, *The Shadow of the Object* (New York: Columbia University Press, 1987), p. 77.
[5] Daniel Stern, *The Interpersonal World of the Infant* (New York: Basic Books, 1987), p. 30.
[6] From Nick Marone, *How to Father a Successful Daughter* (New York: Fawcett, 1988), pp. 28-29.
[7] Daniel Goleman, *Emotional Intelligence* (New York: Bantam, 1995), p. 43.
[8] Thomas Hatch, "Social Intelligence in Young Children," paper delivered at the annual meeting of the American Psychological Association, Washington, D.C., 1990.
[9] Lewis Smedes, *Forgive and Forget* (New York: Pocket Books, 1984), p. 34.
[10] John White, *Eros Defiled* (Downers Grove, Ill.: InterVarsity Press, 1977), p. 18.
[11] Clifford Sager, *Marriage Contracts and Couples Therapy* (New York: Brunner/Mazel, 1976), pp. ix-xi.
[12] R. Larson and M. H. Richards, *Divergent Realities* (New York: BasicBooks, 1994), p. 221.
[13] Jerrold Shapiro, "Letting Dads Be Dads," *Parents,* June 1994.
[14] Dolores Curran, *Traits of a Healthy Family* (New York: Ballantine, 1983), p. 237.
[15] Edith Schaeffer, *What Is a Family?* (Old Tappan, N.J.: Revell, 1975), p. 188.

Chapter 2: A Look at the Story's Authors

[1] James M. Herzog, "Patterns of Expectant Fathers: A Study of the Fathers of a Group of Premature Infants," in *Father and Child,* ed. S. H. Cath, A. R. Gurwitt and J. M. Ross (New York: Blackwell, 1988), p. 303.

[2] Adapted from Froma Walsh, *Normal Family Processes* (New York: Guilford, 1982), p. 176.

[3] Patricia Papernow. *Becoming a Stepfamily: Patterns of Development in Remarried Families* (San Francisco: Jossey-Bass, 1993).

Chapter 3: Your Personal Story Emerges over Time

[1] Stephen Covey, *The Seven Habits of Highly Effective People* (New York: Simon & Schuster, 1989), p. 106.

[2] From Richard Jerome, "Courage at the End of the Road," *People,* August 28, 1995.

[3] Carol Gilligan. *In a Different Voice* (Cambridge, Mass.: Harvard University Press, 1982).

Chapter 4: The Story's Characters

[1] Katie Couric, *The Today Show,* October 12, 1994.

[2] Jerome Bach et al., "A Systems Model of Family Ordinal Position," in John Bradshaw, *Bradshaw On: The Family* (Deerfield Beach, Fla.: Health Communications, 1988).

[3] Walter Toman, *Family Constellation* (New York: Springer, 1969).

[4] S. Watanabe-Hammond, "Blueprints from the Past: A Character Work Perspective on Siblings and Personality Formation," in *Siblings in Therapy: Life Span and Clinical Issues,* edited by M. D. Kahn and G. Lewis (New York: W. W. Norton, 1988), p. 356.

[5] Daniel Goleman, *Emotional Intelligence* (New York: Bantam, 1995), p. 223.

[6] William Wilmot, *Dyadic Communication,* (Reading, Mass.: Addison-Wesley, 1975) p. 45.

[7] Johnny Cash, "I Can Sing of Death, but I'm Obsessed with Life," interview with D. Rader, *Parade,* June 11, 1995, pp. 4-5.

Chapter 5: The Story's Premise

[1] Victoria Secunda. *Women and Their Fathers* (New York: Delta, 1992), p. 287.

[2] Ibid., p. 216.

Chapter 6: The Story's Plot

[1] Ben Patterson, *Serving God: The Grand Essentials of Work and Worship* (Downers Grove, Ill.: InterVarsity Press, 1994), p. 54.

[2] Stephen Covey, *The Seven Habits of Highly Effective People* (New York: Simon & Schuster, 1989), pp. 206-16.

[3] Sue P. Heiney, "The Healing Power of Story," *Oncology Nursing Forum* 22, no. 6 (1995).

[4] David Treadway, "Miniature Roses," *Family Therapy Networker* 18, no. 6 (November/December 1994): 46-64.

[5] Judith Wallerstein and Sandra Blakeslee, *Second Chances* (New York: Ticknor &

Fields, 1989).

[6]Kerian Freeman, "The Hurt with No Name," *Family Therapy Networker* 16 (May/June 1992): 27-31.

Chapter 7: The Story's Dialogue

[1]Daniel Goleman, *Emotional Intelligence* (New York: Bantam, 1995), p. 4.

[2]Ibid., p. 116.

[3]Desmond Morris, *Manwatching* (New York: Abrams, 1977), pp. 83-84.

[4]Ibid., p. 24.

[5]Carolyn Foster, *The Family Patterns Workbook* (New York: Tarcher/Perigee, 1993), p. 194.

[6]Frank Pittman, "No Hiding Place," *Family Therapy Networker* 17 (May/June 1993).

[7]M. J. Mason, "Shame: Reservoir for Family Secrets," in *Secrets in Family and Family Therapy,* ed. E. Imber-Black (New York: Norton, 1993), p. 32. Table used here with permission of W. W. Norton.

[8]Lynn Hoffman, *Foundations of Family Therapy* (New York: BasicBooks, 1981), pp. 108-10.

Chapter 8: The Story's Setting

[1]J. I. Packer, "The Gospel: Its Content and Communication," in *Down to Earth,* ed. John R. W. Stott and Robert Cotte (London: Hodder & Stoughton, 1980), p. 101.

[2]William Strauss and Neil Howe, *Generations* (New York: Morrow, 1991).

[3]Ibid., p. 302.

[4]George Barna, "Generation X vs. Baby Boomers," *InterVarsity,* Winter 1994-1995, pp. 6-7.

[5]Alex Haley, *Roots* (New York: Dell, 1976).

[6]Adapted from Dan Jones, *Words for Our Feelings* (Austin, Tex.: Mandala, 1992), pp. 22-23.

[7]Os Guinness, "The American Cultural Crisis," talk given at Truro Church, Fairfax, Va., 1992.

[8]Robert Bellah et al., *Habits of the Heart* (New York: Harper & Row, 1985).

[9]John Stott, "John Stott Speaks Out," *Christianity Today* 37, no. 2 (February 8, 1993): 37-38.

Chapter 9: The Ongoing Story

[1]Stephen Covey, *The Seven Habits of Highly Effective People* (New York: Simon & Schuster, 1989), pp. 96-97.

[2]Elizabeth Fishel, *Family Mirrors* (Boston: Houghton Mifflin, 1991), pp. 95-96.

Bibliography

Bach, J., et al. "A Systems Model of Family Ordinal Position." In John Bradshaw, *Bradshaw On: The Family.* Deerfield Beach, Fla.: Health Communications, 1988.

Bader, Ellyn, and Peter Pearson. *In Quest of the Mythical Mate.* New York: Brunner/Mazel, 1988.

Bagarozzi, D. A., and S. A. Anderson. *Personal, Marital and Family Myths.* New York: Norton, 1989.

Barna, George. "Generation X vs. Baby Boomers." *InterVarsity,* Winter 1994-1995, pp. 6-7.

Beck, A. T. *Love Is Never Enough.* New York: Harper & Row, 1988.

Beck, A. T., and C. Emery. *Anxiety Disorders and Phobias.* New York: BasicBooks, 1985.

Bellah, Robert, et al. *Habits of the Heart.* New York: Harper & Row, 1985.

Block, Joyce. *Family Myths.* New York: Simon & Schuster, 1994.

Bollas, Christopher. *The Shadow of the Object.* New York: Columbia University Press, 1987.

Boszormenyi-Nagy, Ivan. *Invisible Loyalties.* New York: Harper & Row, 1973.

Bowen, Murray. *Family Therapy in Clinical Practice.* New York: Aronson, 1978.

Bradshaw, John. *Bradshaw On: The Family.* Deerfield Beach, Fla.: Health Communications, 1988.

_____. *Homecoming.* New York: Bantam, 1990.

Cath, S. H., A. R. Gurwitt and J. M. Ross, eds. *Father and Child.* New York: Basil Blackwell, 1988.

Clinebell, H. J., Jr., and C. H. Clinebell. *The Intimate Marriage.* New York: Harper & Row, 1970.

Conway, Jim. *Men in Midlife Crisis.* Elgin, Ill.: Cook, 1978.

Covey, Stephen. *The Seven Habits of Highly Effective People.* New York: Simon & Schuster, 1989.

Curran, Dolores. *Traits of a Healthy Family.* New York: Ballantine, 1983.

Decker, Bert. *You've Got to Be Believed to Be Heard.* New York: St. Martin's, 1992.

Erikson, Erik. *Childhood and Society.* New York: Norton, 1950.

Fishel, Elizabeth. *Family Mirrors.* Boston: Houghton Mifflin, 1991.

Ford, Kevin Graham, with Jim Denney. *Jesus for a New Generation.* Downers Grove, Ill.: InterVarsity Press, 1995.

Ford, Leighton. *The Power of Story.* Colorado Springs, Colo.: NavPress, 1994.

Foster, Carolyn. *The Family Patterns Workbook.* New York: Putnam, 1993.

Fowler, James W. *Stages of Faith.* San Francisco: Harper & Row, 1988.

Freeman, Kerian. "The Hurt with No Name." *Family Therapy Networker* 16 (May/June 1992): 27-31.

Friedman, E. H. *Generation to Generation.* New York: Guilford, 1985.

Goleman, Daniel. *Emotional Intelligence.* New York; Bantam, 1995.

Haley, Alex. *Roots.* New York: Dell, 1976.

Haley, Jay. *Uncommon Therapy.* New York: Norton, 1973.

Heiney, S. P. "The Healing Power of Story." *Oncology Nursing Forum* 22, no. 6 (1995): 899-903.

Hendrix, Harville. *Getting the Love You Want.* New York: Harper & Row, 1988.

Hoffman, L. *Foundations of Family Therapy.* New York: Basic Books, 1981.

Imber-Black, Evan. "Ghosts in the Therapy Room." *Family Therapy Networker* 17 (May/June 1993): 19-29.

_____, ed. *Secrets in Families and Family Therapy.* New York: Norton, 1993.

Jones, Dan. *Words for Our Feelings.* Austin, Tex.: Mandala, 1992.

Kaufman, T. S. *The Combined Family.* New York: Plenum, 1993.

Kelly, Clint. "Me Parent, You Kid! Taming the Family Zoo." *Christianity Today,* January 23, 1995, p. 12.

Larson, R., and M. Richards. *Divergent Realities.* New York: BasicBooks, 1994.

Levin, Pamela. *Cycles of Power.* Deerfield Beach, Fla.: Health Communications, 1988.

Levinson, Daniel. *The Seasons of a Man's Life.* New York: Ballantine, 1978.

Markowitz, L. M. "The Cross-Currents of Multiculturalism." *Family Therapy Networker* 18 (July/August 1994): 18-24.

Marone, Nicky. *How to Father a Successful Daughter.* New York: Fawcett, 1988.

Mason, M. J. "Shame: Reservoir for Family Secrets." In *Secrets in Families and Family Therapy.* Edited by E. Imber-Black. New York: Norton, 1993.

McCoy, Kathleen. *Solo Parenting.* New York: Signet, 1987.

McGoldrick, M., and E. A. Carter. *The Family Life Cycle.* New York: Gardner, 1980.

Miller, Alice. *Prisoners of Childhood.* New York: Farrar Straus Giroux, 1986.

Morris, Desmond. *Manwatching.* New York: Abrams, 1977.

Neuer, Werner. *Man and Woman in Christian Perspective.* Wheaton, Ill.: Crossway, 1991.

Packer, J. I. "The Gospel: Its Content and Communication." In *Down to Earth.* Edited by John R. W. Stott and Robert Cotte. London: Hodder & Stoughton, 1980.

Papernow, P. *A Stepfamily: Patterns of Development in Remarried Families.* San Francisco: Jossey-Bass, 1993.

Patterson, Ben. *Serving God.* Downers Grove, Ill.: InterVarsity Press, 1994.

Pearsall, Paul. *The Power of the Family.* New York: Doubleday, 1990.

Pittman, Frank. "No Hiding Place." *Family Therapy Networker* 17 (May/June 1993):

31-36.

Rader, D. "I Can Sing of Death, but I'm Obsessed with Life." *Parade,* June 11, 1995, pp. 4-5.

Ritchie, Bill. *A Dad Who Will Love You.* Portland, Ore.: Multnomah Press, 1992.

Sager, Clifford. *Marriage Contracts and Couple Therapy.* New York: Brunner/Mazel, 1976.

Satir, Virginia. *Conjoint Family Therapy.* Palo Alto, Calif.: Science and Behavior, 1967.

Schaffer, Edith. *What Is a Family?* Old Tappan, N.J.: Revell, 1975.

Schank, R. C. *Tell Me a Story.* New York: Scribner's, 1990.

Secunda, V. *Women and Their Fathers.* New York: Delta, 1992.

Shapiro, Jerrold. "Letting Dads Be Dads." *Parents,* June 1994.

Shaver, Phillip, and Cindy Hazan. *Psychology Today,* March 1987.

Smedes, Lewis B. *Forgive and Forget.* New York: Pocket Books, 1984.

_____. *Mere Morality.* Grand Rapids, Mich.: Eerdmans, 1983.

Stern, Daniel. *The Interpersonal World of the Infant.* New York: BasicBooks, 1987.

Strauss, William, and Neil Howe. *Generations.* New York: Morrow, 1991.

Toman, W. *Family Constellation.* New York: Springer, 1969.

Treadway, David. "Miniature Roses." *Family Therapy Networker* 18, no. 6 (November/December 1994): 46-64.

Viorst, Judith. *Necessary Losses.* New York: Fawcett, 1986.

Visher, E. B., and J. S. Visher. *Old Loyalties, New Ties.* New York: Brunner/Mazel, 1988.

Wallerstein, Judith S., and Sandra Blakeslee. *Second Chances.* New York: Ticknor & Fields, 1989.

Walsh, Froma. *Normal Family Processes.* New York: Guilford, 1982.

Watanabe-Hammond, S. "Blueprints from the Past: A Character Work Perspective on Siblings and Personality Formation." In *Siblings in Therapy: Life Span and Clinical Issues.* Edited by M. D. Kahn and G. Lewis. New York: Norton, 1988.

White, John. *Eros Defiled.* Downers Grove, Ill.: InterVarsity Press, 1977.

Wilmot, W. W. *Dyadic Communication.* Reading, Mass.: Addison-Wesley, 1975.